# Riding Solo

## How to Embrace being Single and Prepare to find Mr. Right

**Gregg Michaelsen**

DISCLAIMER: As a male dating coach I am very good at what I do
because of my years of studying the nuances of interpersonal
relationships. I have helped thousands of women understand men.

That said, I am not a psychologist, doctor or licensed professional. Do
not use my advice as a substitute if you need professional help.

Women tell me how much I have helped them and I truly hope that I
can HELP you in your pursuit of that extraordinary man! I will provide
you with powerful tools. YOU need to bring me your willingness to listen
and CHANGE!

Congratulations on taking the first step to learning,
understanding and  TAMING men!

# Contents

# Foreword

After spending many years in unhappy relationships myself, I knew it was time to uncover the secret to relationship success. I spent a lot of time researching, talking to people of all ages - some single, some happily married for over fifty years. One thing became abundantly clear. The secret to relationship success isn't what most people think it is. It isn't about having money, living in the right home, or putting the cap on the toothpaste.

Experiencing a truly happy, successful relationship is about first being a successful, independent person. To be one-half of a great relationship, you must first be a confident woman with high self-esteem and self-worth.

Fortunately for me, I grew up with a dad who was a life coach. My whole childhood was filled with having a life coach as a father. By using his techniques on me, he also instilled in me a natural ability to help others in the same way.

At the same time, I am intuitive when it comes to reading people. Within a few minutes of engaging in conversation with someone, I can determine their level of self-esteem and confidence. It was only after years of helping my friends that one of them suggested I get into the business of helping others with their relationships.

What I've noticed in my years of being a dating and life coach is an overarching problem. When a relationship ends, people immediately seek out a new relationship. Men and women both do this and it's not a good thing.

When you're in a relationship, regardless of how long, the end of the relationship leaves you with emotional and physical reactions that work against everything you're about to learn in this book. That's what makes this book so important for you! Your mind desperately wants to experience those happy hormones of love, so it tricks you into pursuing relationships too soon after a breakup.

I knew this book had to be written. I knew I needed to help women feel good about being single. It's time to take away the stigma of being single. It's time to stop looking with pity on someone who is dining alone. It's time to stop jumping into bad relationship after bad. When a relationship ends, your self-confidence and self-esteem drop. You begin to blame yourself for everything that went wrong or, even worse, your former partner blames you.

As you read, you'll learn lots of things about how to embrace being single. You'll learn why it's so important to ditch those self-deprecating thoughts and begin to believe in yourself again. It's time to get to know the wonderful woman who lurks inside of you, and embrace her for exactly who she is.

It's cliché, but today is the first day of the rest of your life. Today, you begin to understand how to end the "date a dud, break up, date another dud" cycle. Today, you begin to build yourself into a strong, confident and independent woman who goes after and chooses great men!

As is always the case, I invite you to reach out to me at **Gregg@ WhoHoldsTheCardsNow.com** if you struggle to understand something you read. I'm not sitting beside you while you read, but I am always here for you.

# *Free Gift!*

It's very important to me that you get the most out of reading this book. In order to help you accomplish that, I have written a companion workbook called *Single Steps*. It is comprised of 30 Single Steps which, when combined with what you read here, will serve to help you inch toward being the confident woman I know you can be!

The workbook is FREE from me to you!
I encourage you to **download it** by going to
**www.whoholdsthecardsnow.com/riding-solo-single-steps/**.

As you read through the book, you will find Action Steps at the end of each chapter. Those Action Steps link directly to your Single Steps in the workbook!

# Introduction

Women email me all the time, desperate for a relationship with a guy - *any* guy. Depending on their age, they may even be willing to settle for just that – *any* guy. They tell me they're miserable and lonely; they just want to be happy again. They're certain that finding a man, *any man*, will do that for them - it will make them happy.

This makes me sad. Why? Because I know the secret to happiness, and it has nothing to do with whether or not I have a girlfriend in my life. I am happy every day, regardless of my relationship status, because I understand that my happiness doesn't come from a relationship, it comes from within.

1

When women tell me they want to find a guy because they're lonely, red flags go up. I know their odds of finding the right guy while they're in this mindset are terrible. Just them telling me this lets me know they're willing to settle for the first guy who comes along. Their standards are lowered to basically any male who is breathing.

The truth is that you need to **embrace being single** when that is, in fact, your relationship status. I know society, and probably your mother, is telling you that you need to get out there and find a guy. They make you think there's something *wrong* with you if you're not in a meaningful relationship. There is a stigma associated with being single.

This is crap!

To add to this, you're miserable because you have convinced yourself that *only* being in a relationship will make you feel happy again. You may feel there is *no way* you can be happy *and* single. It's impossible. This negative self-talk, added to the social stigma and the pressure from friends and family, begins to build. You're feeling so much pressure to date that you'll even date that breathing jerk of a guy who staggered up to you at the bar last week...and you don't even like hanging out at bars!

Come with me on a journey to help you understand three key things:

- Your happiness does not come from being with a guy
- It's okay to be single and female; in fact, if you embrace this status, it can be wonderful!
- Those who embrace being single are the ones who quickly find a great guy!

I know you don't believe me right now, and you may even be thinking of closing the book because you're so skeptical, but I promise that if you hang with me for a while, you will feel much better soon! I will be succinct, I will be informative, and I will be uplifting. Most importantly, I will help you understand and feel better about your circumstance!

Before we move on, I want to quickly examine one important topic: why you're single right now. Stay with me, I have a point. I am not trying to put you down, but I want you to understand some important facts which come with finding yourself single.

If you have just gone through a breakup, it's important for you to understand that your mind and body are going through a chemical withdrawal. This withdrawal is more difficult to overcome than an addiction to cocaine, according to scientific studies (Fisher 2004).

In my book, *He's Gone, Now What?*, I detail all of the reactions your mind and body are having to a breakup. If this is where you are, you might want to stop and read that book first. Otherwise, I can sum it up by saying that the emotional roller coaster you're on right now is completely normal, but with time and some of the tactics you will learn here, you will begin to feel better.

If you are single and have been single for a while, you're probably not going through that chemical withdrawal, but you are still using some pretty hefty negative self-talk, or we wouldn't be spending this time together right now.

Choosing to focus on your career or choosing to put your energy into your children as a single parent are choices you may have made that may have gotten you here. Neither of those is a bad choice. They are valid reasons for not pursuing a relationship. It doesn't make you a bad person or a selfish person, it just makes you human.

You may find yourself now wanting to pursue a relationship, but you have these types of thoughts banging around in your head:

- All the good guys are already taken
- Men my age date much younger women
- I'm too out of practice to make a good girlfriend or wife
- I'm too independent to be in a relationship

While these may seem like valid thoughts, they are railroading your desire to be in a relationship. These inner thoughts are sabotaging your efforts. They all qualify as negative self-talk, and they all hinder what you *think* is your goal of having a great relationship.

Not only that, these thoughts are ideas you've conjured up in your mind. They are not true, but you've come to believe they're true. These are called self-limiting beliefs. You will be learning how to get rid of those very soon!

Before you begin your journey to happiness while single, I want to share with you one very important piece of information. In several studies conducted by Roy Baumeister and others, it was determined that our IQ actually declines when we fear being alone.

In one notable study[1], Baumeister et al tested the IQ of participants and then performed a personality test. After completing these tests, participants were told they were destined to end up alone. Following this brutal revelation, the IQ of the participants was tested again. Their IQ's dropped. The resulting conclusion from these types of studies is that the fear of being alone, or what Baumeister calls anticipated aloneness, actually decreases your level of intelligence.

I was single most of my life. I must be dumb as a brick!

I don't know about you, but that's reason enough for me to think it's time to end the fear of being alone and start working toward being happy while I'm single!

You are under my direction now. I want to take you back to your youth when nothing stopped you from asking questions and growing.

Remember? You asked your parents two thousand questions a day. You couldn't get out of the house fast enough to explore. You talked to anyone. You had confidence.

"Mommy, why is the sky blue?"

"Mommy, why do people yell?"

I would ask the mailman why he drove on the wrong side of his car. He laughed and explained that he had to give me the mail and our mailbox was on the right-hand side of the road, so it made sense for him to be on that side of his car. That wasn't good enough for me. I pointed to my mom's car and told him to fix *his* car.

I was confident because I didn't know better! How perfect!

You know what? You can regain this level of confidence. You can begin right now. Regardless of your age, you can start creating a new story of your life. Your new story will define you. It is a wonderfully exciting story others, including great men, will yearn to hear. Your new story will define your new, confident life. Your new story begins today!

# Chapter 1:
## Let's Examine Being Alone

The word *alone* carries quite a bit of stigma. Nobody wants to use it in a sentence:

- I'm eating *alone* tonight
- I went to the movies *alone*
- I am *alone*
- I live *alone*

Any one of those sentences can be difficult to say aloud, and yet alone has more than one definition. We cling to the negative one.

Let's look at what **Dictionary.com** says about the word *alone*:

> *Alone: separate, apart, isolated from others;*

This is the definition we always assume but what if we took on this one instead:

> *Unique, unequaled, unexcelled*?

Instead of defining yourself based on a negative connotation of the word, why not adopt the more positive meaning? I am unique! I am unequaled!

Ask yourself this: *"Am I willing to settle for someone who isn't right for me just to avoid being alone?"*

I certainly hope the answer is no! Ask yourself this one:

> *"Can I envision my life, the life of my dreams,*
> *if it means I haven't found the man of my dreams yet?"*

Or this one:

> *"Has the lack of a love life caused me to stop loving life?"*

Or:

> *"Am I going to allow the negative thoughts others have put in my mind derail me from finding a truly good man?"*

## Why Is Being Alone So Scary?

When we are children, you rely on someone else to take care of your needs. Someone needs to feed you, change your diapers, and dictate your sleep and wake times. If, as a child, you were left alone, you would be in danger. Over a long enough period of time, you would probably die.

Certainly, as an adult, you no longer need to have someone take care of your basic needs like that. But it is often true that people hand over the care of their physical and/or emotional well-being to their partner. You begin to rely on him for everything. He's your coach and sounding board when you're having a bad day.

Losing that caregiver causes you to feel the same abandonment you would feel as a child, which can make you terribly afraid of loneliness. Valuing and loving *you* has been left to someone else. *You* are no longer doing it.

What has really happened when you feel alone is that you've abandoned yourself. *You* have stopped taking care of your own basic needs – *you* don't value yourself, *you* don't listen to your own thoughts, and *you* don't take care of your physical, emotional or spiritual self. *This* is what is causing you to feel alone. ***You* have abandoned you.**

It's also possible to be in a relationship *and* feel alone. Think back – I bet you've felt that way before. So then, having a man, *any man,* in your life isn't going to make you feel less alone. Have you ever experienced any of these?

- You use anger, blame or tears to control a man
- You allow someone to treat you with intolerable behavior, including physical or emotional abuse
- You've told yourself that, no matter how bad this relationship is, it still beats being alone
- You can't go on with your life if it means being alone

Think back to your last relationship. Weren't there times during that relationship when you felt lonely? Loneliness is a fact of life we must learn to embrace and manage instead of dread. True loneliness comes with a feeling of isolation and emptiness. It's more than wanting to be with someone. It's really about feeling cut off from someone.

Have you ever felt that getting into a relationship to end being alone was a good idea? You're not alone.

## How Can I Stop Feeling So Alone?

### Single Does Not Mean You Are Alone

In order to become a new, confident version of yourself, you need to break some old habits and truly start embracing this time you have alone. That begins when you realize you are **not** alone! You say you are alone because you don't have a boyfriend or husband. I'd argue that your definition of alone is skewed – alone means you are separated, apart or isolated, and you are not any of those things.

Being single is **not** the same as being alone! When I was single, I had more people in my life than I ever had when I was in a relationship. I was far from lonely. In fact, sometimes, I wanted to be alone because I needed a break. Sure, you can wallow in your own misery and stay at home with your cats, but that's your choice. It's a choice I want you to avoid. It's not helping you.

Even though I'm in a relationship, I stay close to my friends. They were the force behind getting me into a relationship! They're part of the team who helped build my great story. I wouldn't be where I am without them. When you decide to enter a relationship, it's important for you to keep your friends around as well.

### A Great First Step

Your first step is to change how you think about being alone. Stop thinking of it as the last resort and start thinking of it as a time to get to know and love yourself. Begin to see your time apart from others as a time of growth and reflection.

My best self-discovery years happened when I was alone. This is when I grew the most as a man. I grew because I took chances and lived outside of my comfort zone. I failed when I tried new things, but instead of giving up, I tried them again and again until I got it right.

I had the confidence and understanding to know that in order to succeed, I would be sure to fail. I had time for experiences which ultimately helped me grow into who I am today because I was alone.

Next, recognize that being alone or feeling lonely isn't permanent. Yes, you might be experiencing this right now, but there are things you can do to promote change. Begin to recognize that you have a problem with being alone and acknowledge your desire to make positive changes.

The healing process may require one-on-one psychotherapy if you feel the need to be around people all the time. Sometimes physical symptoms can give you a clue that something serious is going on. These symptoms often mirror a panic attack and include feeling short of breath, nausea, rapid breathing and heart rate, and sweating.

If you don't fall into that category, you can work on healing yourself by beginning to recognize your perceived flaws and understanding that everyone has flaws. Rather than hiding behind them or pretending they're not there, embrace who you are, flaws and all. Whatever flaws you think you have, I guarantee you have more in strength.

**You are much stronger than you believe you are.**

Do you know what I did in my lonely years? I got a cat, and I named him Tucker! Having someone in the house to talk to, whether they understand you or not, helps take away that feeling of loneliness. You still need to address your fear of loneliness, but having a furry beast who loves you unconditionally can you help you get back on track.

Tucker counseled me for free, well almost. It cost me 14 years of Fancy Feast and kitty litter!

If you don't want to get a pet, you can build your social network, and I don't mean online! In upcoming chapters, you'll learn some great ways to shatter your comfort zone and build your social network.

## Begin to Take Care of Yourself

Throughout this book, you will read a lot about your relationship with yourself. As a woman, you have probably put the care of someone else before your own self-care. Most women are nurturers, but often you nurture others more than yourself.

Taking care of yourself might be a foreign concept to you, or maybe it's just something you once did but now feel you have no time for. It means that at least for a few moments every day or so, you stop the noise of the outside world and breathe in and out.

In my book, *Own Your Tomorrow,* you can learn 14 ways in which you can learn to take care of yourself. These 14 steps also help you learn how to get in touch with who you are and what's going on in your life. You can get a **free** copy of the book by clicking **here**.

## CHAPTER 1 ACTION STEPS

Each chapter contains Action Steps. These are supplemented by the activities in the free companion workbook, *Single Steps*. Watch for links to **download your** *Single Steps* as you proceed through the book.

- Define *alone* differently
- Start taking care of yourself
- Work on changing your internal language

# Chapter 2: Your Emotional Mind

Women are emotional beings. I have three sisters, so I can back this up with personal experience. Man, did I witness the gamut of emotions! This doesn't make you bad people, it just means you're different from men who are usually raised to hold back their emotions and not show them. Honestly, it's tough to decide which is worse: showing emotions as strongly as some women do, or stuffing emotions and pretending they don't exist, as many men do.

My sisters cried and spilled their emotions—I climbed a tree.

The problem with emotions is that we often allow them to bring false truths into our lives. Let me give you an example:

*Sarah is married to Josh, unhappily. They are separated and quite frankly, I don't know why Sarah and Josh ever married except that they have two children together. Soon after their separation, Sarah found Tom and eventually, they moved in together. Not six months later, Sarah and Tom, while still a couple, were not living together any more. Sarah finally realized she needed time alone. Sarah and Josh still do things together with their kids but they're much better apart than they were together. No longer married to Josh, Sarah still sees Tom from time to time, but she has finally allowed herself to face living alone and raising her children by herself.*

Sarah's emotions led her to believe she couldn't survive without living with a man. She has learned to face being alone, but it took bouncing from one bad relationship to another to realize she needed a break. Sarah's thoughts, while she was in this relationship limbo, mostly focused around this one:

*I can't make it on my own.*

Sarah is not unusual. Many women who find themselves stuck in an unhappy relationship are just as afraid as Sarah. Sarah felt her happiness and security were wrapped up in Josh and she couldn't see herself as being happy without a man in her life.

With coaching, Sarah has finally come to understand that she cannot continue to live this way. One of the things we have done is to examine how her negative emotions of fear and apprehension have been impacting her ability to think logically. As she faces being single with fresh eyes, she sees herself making better choices about men.

## We Are of Three Minds

One way of thinking about our emotions is to explore three ways in which our mind works. We have a **Reasonable Mind**, an **Emotion Mind** and a **Wise Mind.** Let's look at each one separately.

### The Reasonable Mind

Your Reasonable Mind is active when you are using logical thought processes. You are thinking things through, formulating a plan and solving problems. You are relying on facts, rather than feelings, to make important decisions. When you are using your reasonable mind:

- You check a movie time at home rather than just showing up at the theater to see what's playing soon
- You plan out your busy day of running errands, rather than just jumping in the car and hoping you get them all done
- You measure ingredients to make cookies, rather than just throwing in some flour, sugar, butter and vanilla
- You study for a test, rather than just showing up and hoping you remember everything

Your reasonable mind has one problem though. It cannot function if your Emotion Mind is triggered. Let's look at the Emotion Mind and then we'll examine why this is true.

### The Emotion Mind

When your emotion mind is working, you do things based on your emotions. You don't think things through and are often impulsive. You find it difficult to think logically, and planning is a big chore. Here are some typical Emotion Mind activities:

- Binge eating and/or drinking
- Taking a trip, on a whim, when you don't have the money
- Buying something because it makes you feel good whether you can afford it or not
- Having a big fight with someone over a small issue
- Being snippy or rude to a sales associate because the store is out of the item you want, *and* are unwilling to wait for it

There is a time when your Reasonable Mind and Your Emotion Mind can work together. In that instance, we say your Wise Mind is at work.

### The Wise Mind

Your wise mind is where reason and emotion come together in a healthy balance. Some call this intuition. It can best be described as a feeling you get that what you're doing is right or the right thing to do.

Some say they physically feel this, "It's a gut feeling." You just know things are how they should be when your Wise Mind is active. The good news is we are all capable of using our Wise Mind, once we find it. To find yours, try these steps.

#### Find a Way to Feel Calm and Peaceful

Often, when your emotion mind is hard at work, you experience stress and anxiety. You know, deep down, you shouldn't be buying those Ugg boots, but it *feels* good. If you go through with buying them, chances are you'll feel some financial anxiety. That $150 could have gone toward the electric bill.

These feelings of stress cause your fight or flight hormones to kick in and you experience:

- A racing heart
- Higher than normal (for you) blood pressure
- Being really moody or agitated
- Feeling overwhelmed or out of control
- Feelings of loneliness, worthlessness and depression
- Difficulty quieting your mind and feeling relaxed
- Being sick more often with colds or infections
- Nausea or upset stomach, diarrhea
- Insomnia

Since none of those sound like much fun, a better idea is to find ways to quiet and calm yourself. It's easier than you think. A great way to bust stress and anxiety is to get some exercise. This might not feel calming at the time, but exercise counteracts those fight or flight hormones and sends them packing.

Another great technique is to close your eyes and take some deep breaths. I like to breathe in and count to myself – one – two – three. Then, I breathe out and repeat it – one – two – three. Repeat this as many times as you need to begin feeling calm. It should happen quickly.

Breathing like this sends a signal to your body that whatever danger it was reacting to is over. Again, those fight or flight hormones are sent packing.

Finding calm and peace is different for everyone. Here are a few other techniques you can try:

- Splash some cold water on your face – this is great if you can't exercise right away
- Take even a ten-minute walk; it's not quite exercise, but it's enough to calm yourself down
- Listen to your favorite type of music
- Play with your pet, or go to an animal shelter or pet store and play with pets there
- Accept where you are in your life, rather than trying to fight it
- Practice mindfulness or focusing on the present moment instead of the future or the past
- Watch a funny movie or show on television

### *Let Go of Intense Emotions (Yes, You Can Do This)*

It's so easy to be angry with someone and hang onto that anger, isn't it? Some women seem to be particularly great at this. When I was in elementary school, a bunch of us boys would play football at recess. One day, this kid Mike kept trying to change the rules so his team could win. We all got really frustrated and quit playing.

Meanwhile, one of my sisters and her friends were experiencing something similar with one of their friends, and they all got angry with that friend.

The next day, the boys and I were playing as if nothing had happened the day before. My sister and her group of friends stayed mad and shunned that friend for a solid two weeks. Now, this is anecdotal for sure, but we both know this is pretty much how it happens.

When you hold onto anger, the person you're angry with isn't impacted. You might say, "*Yes Gregg, yes they are because **I'm** not speaking to them any longer!!*" Okay, but are you sure the other person is negatively impacted by that?

Being angry with someone allows them to live rent-free in your head, replacing positive, calming thoughts with a continual reminder of how this person has wronged you. What would happen if you just let it go? What would happen if you say to yourself, "*I forgive Ann for not including me in her bridal shower*"? You would feel calmer and more peaceful.

In addition, hanging onto that anger means your body is in a continuous state of sensing what it perceives to be dangerous and, once again, you're battling those fight or flight hormones.

I know playing a victim can seem beneficial. Friends and family pour out their sympathy and there is more attention, but is *this* how you want to get their attention? Letting go of pain and anger allows you to calm down and look at life through the lenses of someone who isn't stressed and feeling all those negative things outlined previously. If your pain is deep-rooted, coming from abuse of some form or another, you may need to seek professional help in order to truly let it go, but it's money well spent! Nothing is more important than your mental health.

### How to Let Go of Intense Emotions

#### Learn That Life Doesn't Always Meet Your Expectations

Many times, frustration kicks in when your expectations aren't met. Whether it's an expectation you had of yourself or someone else is immaterial. If we look at relationships, you can experience intense emotions when a relationship you thought was going somewhere suddenly ends.

The emotion probably comes from either anger, disappointment, embarrassment or frustration. While those are valid emotions, they're not productive. The problem is that you had an expectation that was not met. You expected this relationship to go the distance. It didn't.

From here, you have a few choices. You can stuff these bad feelings and move forward, thinking you're okay now. This never works because stuffed emotions always resurface and it's not usually pretty. Your next choice is to allow these emotions to wash over and encompass you. In this scenario, you find yourself wallowing in quart after quart of Ben & Jerrys.

Your third, and I might argue, desirable choice is to feel what you feel *but* recognize that, in the long term, these emotions are *not* productive. Let yourself feel embarrassed. Recognize that your whole world really didn't end and take steps to make a new plan for your life. Let yourself feel angry while allowing yourself to forgive. Forgiveness isn't for the person you forgive. It's for you. It's letting go.

### Invest in the Here and Now, Not the Outcome

Later, you'll learn a little bit about first dates, so I'm not going to spend a lot of time on it now. What I want you to understand right now is that when you go into a relationship expecting that *this one* is **the one**, you are setting all your hopes and dreams on an outcome.

What if, the next time you find someone to date, you spend your time in the here and now. Just enjoy spending time with him without placing an expectation of marriage, living together, or a long-term commitment over your head. Just have fun. Period.

## Shed Your Self-Limiting Beliefs

This is another topic you'll study in-depth later in this book. A self-limiting belief is something you tell yourself, but it holds you back. *"I could never dive off of the high dive"* is a self-limiting belief. Sometimes, they aren't that obvious.

We all have self-limiting beliefs. Getting rid of them will help you move toward happiness in your life.

## End the Control Game

Have you ever had someone in your life who wanted to control your every move? Maybe a parent, a best friend, or a partner in a relationship? Maybe you've even held that role at some point.

Here's the problem with this notion of controlling someone else. You can't do it. Nope. No way. You can control *you,* and that's it. Of course, many people don't believe this either. You can control your thoughts and feelings by recognizing them when they crop up and managing them. If you're feeling frustrated, you don't need to let that take control. You can dig in and ask yourself, *"Why am I frustrated?"* Dig until you find the answer, and then deal with it. You might have a perfectly good reason for being frustrated, but that doesn't mean you can't do something to lift your emotions. If you learn to control yourself, that will be good enough for any great man!

## Let Go of Worrying About What "Everyone Else Thinks"

Oh boy. This one is a doozy. You don't dance at the party because you worry about what everyone will say. You wear certain styles of clothing so 'people won't talk'. You don't hang out with specific friends in public because they're slightly different from you and you don't want someone to get the wrong idea about you.

Imagine a world where you didn't care what other people thought about what you're doing. How freeing do you think that would be? I've got a secret for you. It's brutal but you can handle it. Ready?

Nobody cares what you're doing but you. *Everyone else* is doing the same thing you are - worrying about what others think. This is a low-confidence thought process, and it's one that must go. If you want to dance, dance. If someone criticizes you for it, laugh it off and say something back like, *"Well, I know I look like a goof out there, but I'm having fun, and that's all that counts!"* Let them scratch their heads on that.

As you proceed, you will learn other ways of letting go of your intense emotions. I could go on and on here, but it would be repetitive. Just keep reading and you'll get it!

### Acknowledge Feelings of "This Is Just Right" or "This Is the Right Thing to Do" – Gut Feelings

Somewhere deep down inside, even though we all do things we know we shouldn't, there is a voice saying, *"You shouldn't be doing this."* Too often, that little voice gets drowned out by this one, *"It will be fine. You can always find a way to borrow money for rent. Just buy the shoes."*

Of course, if you're like me, not ten minutes after you ignore the voice saying, *"You shouldn't do this,"* you're left feeling terrible, maybe even anxious, and there you are, back on the anxiety hamster wheel again.

Another way in which this might creep up is when you're engaging in an activity you know will have a negative impact on your health like smoking, drinking excessively or doing drugs. Somewhere deep inside, you know this isn't right, but an overwhelming feeling of anxiety, depression or low self-worth is pushing back harder, and you do it anyway.

Sometimes, to deal with this, we exercise something called cognitive dissonance. I'll use smoking to explain it. When you smoke, you know it's harmful to your health, but time after time, you've been to the doctor and left with a clean bill of health. It's not harmful to *your* health, you tell yourself. You may also justify it by saying it calms your nerves, therefore it's worth the risk.

Cognitive dissonance is when you know what you're doing is wrong, but you find a way to justify it to yourself. A friend of mine is struggling with her mother's negativity. Recently, the mom said, *"You really need to go up a size in pants."* As soon as my friend turned and glared at her mother, her mother justified the statement, *"Don't you want me to tell you so you don't go out in public like that?"*

The truth was my friend looked fine. In fact, she had lost about ten pounds and the pants were a little loose on her. Her mother knew the statement she was delivering was hurtful, but she outwardly justified it, not only to herself but to her daughter as *helpful*. That's cognitive dissonance. The trick is catching yourself when you do it, so you can stop and acknowledge the thing you're doing *before* you do it, so it doesn't cause you angst.

### *Look at How You Feel After a Crisis Situation –*
### *Note the Calm After the Storm You May Feel*

You just got a phone call that your dad was taken to the ER with chest pain. You drop what you're doing and rush off to be with your family. Your stress level is through the roof, and those fight or flight hormones have kicked into high gear.

You get to the hospital, and, after waiting for what seems like forever, you get the all-clear. Dad was suffering from a severe case of indigestion after eating too much Mexican at lunch today.

What happens next? Do you ever pay attention? You probably feel like all the tense air that was holding your body up just drains out of you. You might even outwardly heave a huge sigh. The racing heart, sweating and other symptoms of high adrenaline suddenly flee your body, and you feel calm.

While the situation itself wasn't so hot, feeling calm and peace afterward is great. This is what you're shooting for. That letting out of all the stress-filled air. The depletion of your anxious energy. A feeling that all is right in the world, at least for now.

### Notice When You Suddenly See Something in a New Way That Just Seems to Make Sense to You

Have you ever just been perplexed by something? Long division? Calculus? Chemistry? How your car engine works? How to redecorate your living room?

Then, suddenly, that thing becomes clear. You finally figure out long division. You 'get' calculus. Someone explains your car engine to you in a way you understand, or you finally find the living room you want on Pinterest.

Isn't that a great feeling? It's another heavy sigh moment, depending on the importance of what you just figured out. Not knowing something can be very frustrating, and depending on what it is you don't know and how important it is in your life, it can be stressful.

Figuring it out, solving the puzzle, is such a rewarding feeling. You might even get a bit of an emotional high from it. Think back to tests you took in high school or college. You know the ones. You thought you completely bombed the thing. You're expecting an "F" on it, but when you get it back, you managed to get a "C." You realize you understood the material better than you thought. It makes sense to you.

I know you're happy now! I would be!

### Why Emotional Thinking Often Overrides Logical Thinking

Have you ever bought something like an expensive pair of shoes or a new television, and then, several hours or days later, wondered what the heck you were thinking and regretted the decision?

In this instance, your emotional mind was in full gear, and your logical or reasonable mind was not able to surface. Maybe you were super anxious about something. You could have been sad for some reason or another. The reason for the high emotion doesn't much matter.

When you are highly emotional, ideas or feelings are often distorted into truths or made more important than they should be.

When there isn't a balance between emotional mind and reasonable mind, you might make regrettable decisions. Decisions should be made when you don't feel like the world has just come crashing down on you, or conversely, like you just won the lottery.

When you're considering a large purchase, or you find yourself in an argument, step back and take some deep breaths. Allow your emotions to back off so some logic can enter the scene. I know. Easier said than done.

I made a pact with myself; I don't make any major decision when I am emotional. I know better. It can wait. Let the decision sit for a day or two and then revisit it.

## Self-Soothing

We live in a world where many people believe they cannot feel comforted unless someone else comforts them; they are unable to self-soothe. I won't get into the many reasons why this happens but suffice it to say you learn to self-soothe early in your life. The good news is that, even as an adult, you can still learn some great techniques to soothe yourself and reach that Wise Mind of yours.

Self-soothing is all about being kind to yourself and learning to calm yourself down when you're over the edge emotionally. You don't need expensive tools to soothe yourself. You just need to take advantage of something you already possess – your five senses.

### *Soothe Visually*

One of my favorite things to do is look outside my back door at the nature behind my condo. Sometimes, I even head out for a walk so I can truly appreciate what's there. This is a great activity to calm or soothe yourself. Whether you decide to look at nature through a window or on your computer, or you opt to take a walk in the woods, on the beach, or down your favorite street, you are engaging in a self-soothing activity.

If you don't like nature, you can do other things which signify beauty to you; visit a museum or an observatory, maybe an arboretum or an art gallery. Whatever you find beautiful will work. Once you're there, just enjoy being there. Shut out the bad! Focus on just being where you are and forget about what's coming in the future or what's happened in the past.

Take in each thing you see and just be present with that paint-ing, flower or tree. Let go of all your negative thoughts if they come along, and just enjoy being where you are right then.

A great technique some like to use is visual meditation. There are tons of great videos on YouTube that will walk you through this, but you don't need a video. You can just close your eyes and imagine yourself somewhere calming like a beautiful garden or a beach in Hawaii. Wherever your happy place is, imagine yourself there.

A few other ideas for visual soothing:

- Light a candle and watch the flame dance
- Sit in a garden and look at all the beautiful flowers
- Watch it snow or rain
- Watch the birds flying around to make their nests
- Buy a flower and put it where you can see it often
- Watch fish swim in an aquarium

### Soothe by Listening

Another favorite activity of mine is to listen to a thunderstorm. I don't know what it is about them, but I just love listening the raindrops hit the window or roof. Getting lost in the repetitive-ness of the raindrops helps me to focus on that versus whatever negative thoughts might have started to run through my mind (yes, I have them too, sometimes).

Some great, soothing listening activities you can try include:

- Listen to beautiful or soothing music like nature sounds, or pretty much any meditation or yoga type music

- Listen to the sound of a baby cooing, laughing or gurgling
- Sit near a waterfall or find that sound on your phone and play it
- If you don't live near a waterfall, try listening to the sound of a stream or river as the water rushes over the rocks and bangs up against the soil
- Listen to other repetitive noises like someone chopping wood

When you are listening to these sounds, just let them wash over you. Let them come and go, just as you let your thoughts and emotions come and go. Sink into a relaxing position and just listen.

### Soothing Smells

Many realtors will tell clients to bake cookies before a house showing to put a calm and welcome smell in the home. Baking a favorite treat is a great way to self-soothe. The smell of chocolate chip cookies soothes me. It might be brownies or coffee for you.

A few other ways you can use smell to soothe yourself:

- Sit in a fragrant garden; close your eyes and just smell the beauty
- Smell the rain; there is no other smell like it
- Light a scented candle or burn some incense
- Go somewhere where they cook your favorite foods, and take in the smells of bacon and eggs or steak – then eat them

It is noteworthy that one of our greatest memory triggers is smell. Be careful when choosing a smell not to choose one which will stir negative memories... like when I choked on popcorn.

### Tasty Treats to Soothe

If you love chocolate brownies, get yourself one and savor every bite. Eat it slowly and truly be in the moment – taste the chocolate and enjoy it. I'm not saying binge on the whole tray of brownies, but I'm not one who believes in depriving yourself of something as some form of *diet*. Everything in moderation.

If you're trying to let go of sweets, make your favorite meal. One final taste you might enjoy is some herbal tea or hot chocolate. Both have soothing effects and the warmth is always calming.

### Soothing Touches

And last, but not least, you can self-soothe with touch. Who doesn't love touching something like a big furry blanket or a silk shirt? Try either one the next time you feel like you need to just chill. If you're an animal lover, like me, try petting a dog, cat, bunny, or another furry critter. There is something very calming about petting an animal, and most of them won't fight you on it either. I would, however, avoid a skunk!

You can sink into your comfy bed or snuggle up in a warm cozy blanket to calm down. You could take a swim and let the water just flow over your body.

One final way to use touch as a soother is to find a heavy blanket and lay under it. Let it envelop you and imagine the feeling of big, loving arms wrapped around you. This is often a therapeutic tool for people with anxiety. The weight of the blanket is key – make it heavy enough to feel comforted.

## Wrapping Up

Any of the activities we have touched upon in this chapter may work to help you manage your emotions when they are running amok. The main way in which these work is by taking your focus from your thoughts to something real in front of you – whether it's something sensory or an activity.

This distraction helps you shake free of the emotional downer and refocus on the beauty around you, even if you pipe it in on your phone. Once your emotions are settled, you can now get back to writing the version of your story that will make you happy – the right way – from within!

---

### CHAPTER 2 ACTION STEPS

- Begin to take note of which mind you think you're using: reasonable, emotional or wise

- Try some of the self-soothing activities you've read about and see what works for you

---

# Chapter 3:
## Flawed Thinking Habits

A quick scour of the internet provides multiple references to information stating that the average person is believed to have between 12,000 and 70,000 thoughts every day. As many as 70% of those are negative thoughts. If we believe this statistic, and there isn't anything to tell us not to, this means up to 49,000 thoughts every day are negative, leaving just 21,000 positive thoughts. Holy cow!

Do you understand what this means? We are spending, or rather wasting, about 70% of our time in a negative headspace. Our inner game is working against us 70% of the time. That's no joke. Here is the larger problem – we take the majority of those thoughts and randomly, without validation, turn them into facts.

*I will never meet a great guy.*

*I can't survive life with kids on my own.*

*All the great guys my age are taken.*

*No guy will ever like me.*

*I'm too (insert fat, ugly, stupid, etc.) for any guy to love me.*

Rather than taking these as they are – thoughts – we assume them to be true and assign them great importance in our daily lives. Once you take, *I will never meet a great guy,* and turn it into a fact, rather than what it was, a random thought, you've made a false decision about your life that you will now ruminate over---forever.

## Rumination

Perhaps the worst part of turning thoughts into false facts is what happens to them after we assume them to be true; we ruminate on them. What is rumination[2]?

*Rumination is a type of obsessive overthinking in which a person will mentally replay a past negative event again and again but make no real progress toward resolution.*

What this means is that your mind takes a negative thought like, *all my relationships ended because I'm too fat and ugly,* and you make it a fact. From there, you begin to think *only* about that fact. You turn it over and over, obsessing over it. Your whole focus becomes what you believe to be a fact - you're too fat for any guy to love.

Just to play Devil's Advocate here, let's assume you *are* overweight. All you are doing by ruminating is staying stuck on the fact that you're overweight. You might be focused on a cause like childhood abuse, a parent who comforted you with food or a host of other causes. You are focused on the perceived consequences – no man will ever love me. BUT, are you focusing *any* energy on finding a solution?

I had a reader call me fat a few months ago. She called me ugly too! The truth is that I wasn't fat, well maybe a little, but she gave me a kick in the butt. I changed my eating habits, doubled down on my workout routine, and lopped off 20 pounds. I feel better. Not because I felt fat before, but because I started taking better care of myself.

Now I am working on the ugly part. Haha!

If feeling fat is your rumination point, *do something* about it. Get up and move. Take a walk, go to the gym, find a friend and challenge one another to hit so many steps per day or walk so many miles. Don't just sit there and fret over what's wrong. **Take action:** you will feel awesome afterward!

My motivation for change was a stranger calling me fat. I could have gotten upset. Instead, I am strong enough, through what I'm now teaching you, to do something about it!

Now there are times where you can't so easily change what you perceive to be wrong, and sometimes what you're ruminating over is something outside of your control.

Let's look at another example:

*All of the great guys my age are taken.*

Is this really true? Have you looked and found that there are **no men** in your age bracket who are single and available? Of course not. There *are* single men available in any age bracket you want. I coach women in their 70's who are actively dating. The real truth is that you've convinced yourself this thought is a fact, and now you're stuck in believing it.

### Why do We Ruminate?

For many of us, we ruminate because it's human nature to do so. As our brains and minds have evolved, protective measures have been put into place. Considering the negative possibilities is one of those protective measures. Suppose you live in the dinosaur days. You're out, hunting for dinner, when **BAM,** a t-rex heads your way. Your mind immediately shoots to the negative possibilities and you run like heck back to the safety of your cave.

The problem is that we have not evolved past this need for such danger preparedness. As a result, we downplay the positives in our lives and magnify the negatives that scare us so we can protect ourselves.

For some, rumination occurs due to a strong need for approval by others. You found a guy you liked online and sent him a message. He didn't reply for who knows what reason, but if you are fixated on being *too fat*, you might make a wrong assumption that he took one look at your photo, decided you were too fat and moved on. The truth is you have no idea why he didn't reply. Maybe *he* is the loser, or perhaps he found someone else.

Another example would be a friend who has a New Year's Eve party every year, and you've been invited for the past several years, but this year, no invitation came. You assume she no longer likes you and just didn't invite you. The facts in either of these circumstances are most likely *not* what you assume them to be.

Maybe the online guy thought *he* was too… something… to date a great woman like you – maybe *he* was a shy geek afraid to be rejected. Maybe he found you to be so beautiful, he was intimidated by you! I bet that one never crossed your mind! It should! Perhaps your friend isn't even having a party this year. The facts are irrelevant, you just know you got tossed, and you assume it's because of you.

For many people who ruminate, the cause is low self-worth. You assume that every negative thing someone else tells you about yourself is true, and you assume everything your mind conjures up is true as well.

I was told I was fat and ugly – should I take this as fact?

*Why do I keep failing with men?*

You may take a relationship failure and place all the blame squarely on your own head. Of course, the truth is that he was probably not right for you for one reason or another. Maybe your values weren't properly aligned, or maybe he turned out to be a cheater. Maybe you wanted kids and he didn't. Maybe you simply don't understand how men think.

This doesn't mean *you* failed, it means the relationship wasn't meant to be. Period. However, if you have low self-worth, you can be pretty good at taking on all the blame by yourself and further berating yourself.

The irony is he's probably thinking that *he* is to blame!

A final cause for rumination is stress and/or anxiety. Anxious moments come when we take a situation that will happen in the future and we envision a negative ending.

*When I go to meet up with this guy I met online, he will see that my eyes are too far apart, my knees are knobby, and I am overweight. He won't like me and might not even come up to me - then there I will be, sitting in a restaurant all by myself. It will be obvious to **everyone** that I got stood up. **How embarrassing!***

Now, you're already anxious about the date because it's a first date, and first dates go hand-in-hand with being anxious. But, since you've ruminated on all of your flaws for a while now, you've inserted them into your anxiety and made it ten times worse.

For all you know, this guy likes women whose eyes are set apart, who have knobby knees and who are a little overweight. Chances are *you* won't show up for the date and if you do, you'll be waiting for him to pull some stunt like going to the bathroom and exiting out the back door.

### How Can I Stop Ruminating?

The first thing to understand about rumination is that our minds are accustomed to these negative thoughts. A neural network has been formed to support negative thoughts. Reversal is possible, but you *must* put in the work!

This neural network you've developed is triggered by your mood, so when you're ruminating, you're in that negative mood and bingo, neural network triggered and you're off. In order to reprogram these networks, think of a time when you were afraid, and something worked out as it should have. This might take some work on your part. If we stick with the first date example, think of a time when you went on a first date and the guy showed up, he was nice, and the evening was fun. This should trigger a happier memory.

If you need help, turn to your friends and family. They are much more likely to remember your successes and positive events than you are. Another tool is to get out your phone, or if you're old enough to have one, your photo album. Look at photos from happy times. Look at those photos of your high school prom where you had a good time. Look at photos of you and a guy you dated having fun together. Not *all* dating scenarios are bad.

Music is a great memory trigger. What types of music, or what musicians, trigger happy memories for you? As you use these triggers, you're not looking at the ultimate outcome of the relationship, but at that happy moment.

What is important to remember is that you are reprograming those neural networks by taking a fear and remembering a time when things *did* work out. The more you do this, the less likely you will be to turn to rumination.

And yes, you *have* had a ton of successes in your life; don't tell me differently! Success comes in all shapes and sizes. It can be getting an "A" on a difficult exam. It could be landing your first job after college, or your first job *ever* when you were a teen. It might be passing a difficult certification exam for your profession or doing a great job on a report. Success can be learning to ride a bike, learning to drive, or learning to paint with oils and acrylics. It can be speaking in public for the first time, speaking to a stranger, or choosing a great outfit for your first day on a new job.

### Finding a Solution

It's important to remember that when you are in an emotional state, i.e. ruminating, you cannot logically come up with a solution to your dilemma. Recall our discussion on Reasonable, Emotion and Wise Mind in chapter two. By recalling a positive outcome to the same type of trigger, you are enabling yourself to begin logically problem-solving the thing about which you're stressing.

Once you have begun to turn the negative rumination into positive memory journeys, it's time to begin putting the anxiety to rest. Remember, your mind is not capable of problem-solving when you are in an emotional state, so you need to get to a happy place before you can find a solution.

Your first step is to spend ten to fifteen minutes, and no more, writing down the things you ruminate over. Don't start actually ruminating, just make a list of the things you worry about. Your list might look something like this:

- I am overweight
- My financial life is in ruins
- No guy will find me attractive
- My car is sure to die any day now
- My boss hates me

Now, take those items and look for connections between them. Do any of them connect in any way? You might say that being overweight connects to not being attractive to men. You could also say that your financial life being in ruins loosely connects to worrying about your car dying on you.

Take each problem, or set of problems, now and begin to brainstorm a solution. If you're overweight, what can you do about it? If your financial life is in ruins, what's a solution? If you're afraid your car is close to the end of its life, how can you resolve this?

When you come across things like "My boss hates me" or "No guy will find me attractive," you might not see a solution, but you also need to ask yourself one important question – is this true? If you truly believe your boss hates you, what can you do about it? Why might s/he not like you? Is your work sub-par? Does s/he feel threatened by the possibility of you taking his/her job? In any of those instances, what can you do to fix it?

- Stay calm
- Break each issue down by providing small steps each day to fix the problem
- Take action each day, starting with the easiest
- Realize that some days you may go backward, but the next day you will likely move forward again; backward is normal as long as you don't let it bring you down
- Notice how great you feel when you take even a few baby steps
- Reward yourself for taking action instead of ruminating!
- Keep going

You'll find your confidence will start to go in the right direction.

## Begin to Observe Your Thoughts

For any of this to work for you, I would like you to become an observer of your thoughts. I made a coaching client very angry once when I told her she could control her thoughts. She whole-heartedly believed this was not true. She was ruminating over a breakup and the last thing she wanted to hear was that she was ultimately in control of her own thoughts.

Your thoughts are there, and yes, they do seem to randomly come and go, **but** that doesn't mean you can't do something with them when they arrive. If you're following the **Single Steps** in the free workbook, you've already started writing down negative thoughts. Start looking back through these, and make sure you're doing something to turn them around.

## Your Past Might Be Your Undoing

I often tell my readers that the rejection they've suffered throughout their lifetimes has harmed their self-esteem. I wonder if they believe me, or if they think this doesn't apply to them. Well, not to get too science-y on you here, but another study, conducted by one of Baumeister's cohorts, Tyler Stillman, produced results[3] to back me up.

Stillman's study, which involved college-age students, paired people up, by video, with partners. The students were told they were participating in an experiment about first impressions. Some students were told that their video partner decided not to meet with them. Others, the control group, were not given this information.

The students who felt rejected by their partners felt a measurable decline in their sense of purpose and self-worth. Think online dating...

You send an email, a wink, poke, or whatever to some guy you like online. Perhaps he even emails or winks back. Then nothing. How do you feel? Rejected right? Of course! We have an innate need to connect with others, so when someone seems to be moving toward us but then suddenly moves away, we feel rejected. When this person disappears without explanation, you feel invalidated. You feel dismissed, ignored, and unimportant.

The problem is that when you feel like this, your ability to make good choices and feel life is meaningful is depleted. It doesn't even matter if your rejection comes from a potential date or someone else. It could be that you tried to strike up a conversation with a stranger on the train into work, but they kept their nose in their phone the whole time, ignoring you.

These situations leave you feeling that rejection. In addition to making poor choices, you might find yourself giving up on difficult or frustrating tasks more quickly. It can cause you to have difficulty managing your emotions, which you just learned is very important to logical thought.

## There Is Nothing Wrong with You!

Just because you are struggling to find a happy relationship with a guy doesn't mean you're flawed in some way. It means you may need to change a few things, but it doesn't mean you're broken beyond repair, regardless of what your mind is telling you.

### We are our own worst enemies!

When is the best time to make these changes? You guessed it – when you are single.

Chances are, you simply need a reboot. Many of the women I coach tell me they feel very confident in other areas of their lives, but in their dating life, they feel very low confidence. This isn't something you're doing wrong, it's just a result of your past catching up with you.

Crawl out of this low-confidence mode into a high-confidence place where you're not ruminating, you're self-soothing, you're staying in the moment, and you're using your reasonable or logical mind *and* your emotional mind together to make sound, thoughtful decisions. Now, you are in the proper mindset to fix the problem with these steps:

- Stay calm
- Break each issue down by providing small steps each day to fix the problem
- Take action each day, starting with the easiest
- Realize that some days you may go backward, but the next day you will likely move forward again; backward is normal as long as you don't let it bring you down
- Notice how great you feel when you take even a few baby steps
- Reward yourself for taking action instead of ruminating!
- Keep going

Piece of cake!

---

### CHAPTER 3 ACTION STEPS

- Recognize your successes in life
- Keep observing and modifying your negative thoughts

# Chapter 4: Create Your Vision & Live the Part!

We all have some core beliefs. These beliefs focus on several areas of your life such as power, love, sex, friendship, spirituality, men, and so on. In addition, you probably have some reality you cling to about your life. This reality is developed based on what you believe and your personal experiences. Sometimes, those realities form based on what you think you should do, rather than on what you want to do.

You work at a job you hate because you should pay the bills. Of course, you should pay the bills, but what if your job was the job you really want? Even if you have to take a pay cut, would you do it? If it meant you were happy, would you at least consider it?

Sadly, some will shake their heads no at these questions. I'm lucky. The work I do every day is work I love. I am excited to get up each morning and face what's coming that day.

The question I have for you, right now, is whether or not you even *know* what you want in your life. Have you ever thought about what you *want?* Have you ever spent even a few moments dreaming of the life you could have if there were no roadblocks? At the end of this chapter, you'll have a *Single Step* activity to do to help you think this through.

## A Funny Thing Happened on the Way to My Dream

When I talk about dreams and goals, people will listen, but they don't take the steps to actually generate positive change in their life. This isn't you! I *dare* you to live a life of mediocrity! I challenge you to remain stagnant.

See how ridiculous it sounds?

You can do better. You can be a better mother, girlfriend, friend, daughter, boss and coworker. What is it going to take for you to feel motivated to make the changes that will propel you forward in your life? It will take trying things you've never tried before and failing more times than you want to.

If you allow yourself to do these things, you will gain many new, and often fun, experiences. You will learn to embrace failure and see it instead as an opportunity to grow and learn. You will meet many new friends, and ultimately, you will build your confidence.

A funny thing happens on the way to realizing your dreams. You develop self-worth, higher self-esteem and greater confidence. You begin to realize your goals and dreams. You begin to believe in yourself, and you start to see that you *can*.

All I am asking of you as you continue through this book and your *Single Steps* is to change your attitude and your perception of what you *think* you know. Allow time in your life to become an adventurer. Explore what you think is true about yourself. Expand your horizons. Unveil the adventurer who lies within. Allow her to shine and explode your life into something truly wonderful!

## Time to Recognize Limiting Beliefs

Why do you think you either don't know what you want out of your life or haven't yet pursued your dreams? It's not because you aren't capable. Don't tell me that because I won't believe it, not even for a moment! I've got a better answer!

Your limiting beliefs are holding you back!

Let's look at a limiting belief. I like to use power. Like me, you hold some belief about power. Perhaps you believe that power is indicative of meanness because someone who held power over you in your past was mean.

If you seek to become a powerful person, maybe a leader, this belief will keep you from your dream. Let's look at how the thought process goes.

I want to be powerful ⇨ Powerful people are mean ⇨ I don't want to be mean ⇨ I can't be powerful.

This is a simplistic way of looking at it, but this is an example of a self-limiting belief. You have created a reality based on a flawed belief. Do you know any powerful people who are *not* mean? I'm sure you do. Think of a teacher you favored or a boss you thought was great. Those were people with power over you, and they debunk your belief.

The easiest way to find your limiting beliefs is to look at your dreams and determine which of them you feel are most unattainable. Even if you're practicing positive self-talk, limiting beliefs can lurk beneath the surface. Of course, I've got a *Single Step* activity to help you through the process.

Let's look at an example.

Suppose you're worried about money. How does this stress make you feel? Probably anxious, maybe angry because you feel like you can't catch a break. You might feel hopeless that your situation will never get any better.

Now, sit with some of those feelings. If you feel anxious about not having enough money, what's the real pressure point? *"What will my family think if I can't make it on my own?"* or, *"If I can't live in this expensive neighborhood, people will think less of me."*

Your limiting beliefs in this example might be focused on people thinking less of you because you're struggling financially. Maybe if you're angry, you're thinking something like, *"Life isn't fair."* Hopelessness might go something like, *"I will never be able to get my head above water – I'm not smart enough to figure it out."*

## Getting Rid of Limiting Beliefs

Once you start to identify some of your limiting beliefs, it's time to start getting rid of them.

Start by taking one of your limiting beliefs and writing it, by itself, on a piece of paper. Just sit and look at it. How does it make you feel? Angry? Sad? Anxious? Fearful? How strong are these feelings? Write all of this down with your belief.

*I can't make enough money. I get strong feelings of fear and anxiety when I read this statement.*

Now, it's time to face the truth versus this belief.

It could be that you believe you can't make enough money because you don't think you're smart enough, you didn't go to college, or someone has told you this in the past.

Is this really true? There are *many* people who have made more than enough money without a college education. In fact, it's often true that blue collar jobs pay better, especially when you're younger. There is also rarely a true dead-end job, and many places of employment will help you pay for the added education you need to advance.

I know it's hard to change this belief, but in order to change your course, you must change your belief.

Your next step is to replace this limiting belief with a better one. For example, *"I can make enough money if I find a second job." Or, "I can have enough money if I cut back on my expenses."* Even better is, *"My financial problems of the past have taught me some valuable lessons and I am prepared to put those lessons to use now."*

Your last step is to now look at that new statement. How does it make you feel? Energized? Hopeful? Excited? Motivated? I bet it does. My point here is that before you can solve the issue, be it happiness or your finances, you must turn your negative thought patterns into positive ones.

Do this and the magic begins. The solutions start to become clear!

## Your Beliefs About Being Single

Now, it's time for the fun part. Think hard about your beliefs regarding singlehood. You may have already uncovered some or all of them. This really shouldn't be too difficult because you bought this book based on a limiting belief. Why did you purchase this book? Complete this sentence:

> "*I hate being single because...*"

If you have more than one response to fill in that blank, take them one at a time. Write each one down on a sheet of paper. Study it, think about how it makes you feel inside. Do you feel angry? Frustrated? Hopeless? Encouraged? Rejected? Label your feelings about your limiting belief.

Now, build a new belief that is not limiting. I'll give you an example:

> "*I hate being single because it confirms to me that nobody wants me.*"

Your new belief could be:

> "*There is someone out there for me, and I will find him soon.*"

Let's try another:

> *"I am too fat for anyone to love me."*

Let's fix it:

> *"I am going to start working out so I can be healthy for me, and not anyone else."*

Now that you've rewritten one or more of your limiting beliefs into new beliefs, take each one and look at it. How does it make you feel? Again, you should have some positive emotions.

## Live the Part

There is one more step in this process of eliminating your self-limiting beliefs.

> *Start living your life based on your new belief.*

Whether you truly believe this new statement or not is irrelevant at this point. Force your mind to latch onto something new. The best way to do that is to act like it's already true.

For example, if your limiting belief was that you're too fat for anyone to love you, you need to start acting like the thinner version of yourself you dream of. Where does she go? What does she do during the day? How does she eat? Who are her friends? What does her wardrobe look like? Does she hang out at the pool in a swimsuit?

Some of these actions will take true courage on your part. It is facing that fear of jumping out of an airplane that helps you overcome it. It's wearing that swimsuit at the pool, not caring what others think, that gives you the courage and gumption to try something bolder!

Now, obviously, you need to be reasonable. If your limiting belief is financial and your new belief is having the money to do what you want, you can't just go willy-nilly and start spending money you don't have, but you could build a vision board which represents the things you want to have, do, or be when your finances are in order.

## One More Thing

You've created a life centered around your limiting beliefs. Depending on how old you are, these beliefs may have been part of your life for decades. We build the life we have based on what we believe.

If you believe you're not good enough, you won't be motivated to try. Others who do believe in you will label you as an under-achiever. You might work a job well below your true potential. You may not manage your finances because you've already decided you'll live a life of paycheck-to-paycheck stress. You probably won't have many friends or be motivated to go out and meet new people. Your lifestyle validates your beliefs, and you even say things like, "*See! I've been stuck in this entry-level job for ten years! I told you I wasn't good enough!*"

Turning your entire lifestyle around is something I know you can do! I believe in you! It will be scary! I am not going to lie to you. There may be days you wake up scared to death at the plan you made, but you must push yourself forward. Face those fears and be brave enough to make the changes I know you're capable of.

My mom is befuddled by me. I never read. In fact, the last book I read was *Charlotte's Web* in 4th grade! I'm kidding, but that's not far from the truth. My three older sisters read everything. My mom can't believe that *I* became the writer in the family.

Did I have limiting beliefs? I sure did. But I overcame them. I threw them out the window because they were hurting me. I just started writing because one day I decided I could, and I liked it. Am I smarter than you? I highly doubt it. **I know you can overcome your self-limiting beliefs, too!**

Now, do you see the power you gain when you throw those beliefs away?

If you're stuck in an entry-level job, go back to school or seek the training you need to move up. It might be as simple as applying for a promotion or changing companies. You don't need to live paycheck to paycheck either. Get a second job or cut back on your expenses. There are always things you can do to make positive changes. You just have to set your mind to doing them and kill off those limiting beliefs.

These changes won't happen overnight and simply saying to yourself, "*I am thin*" doesn't make you so. Regardless of the belief you need to turn around, there is hard work to be done, but the payoff is so enormous that it's well worth the effort!

---

### CHAPTER 4 ACTION STEPS

- Begin identifying what it is you really want out of your life
- Start uncovering your self-limiting beliefs so you can begin to overwrite them with truth

---

# Chapter 5: It's Time to End the Madness!

*Whether you think you can, or you think you can't*
*— you're right.*

That quote is from Henry Ford, a great American innovator of his time. What it really means is that your attitude is everything. If you believe in yourself, you can accomplish great things. If you don't believe in yourself, you will struggle to accomplish the things you want in your life.

Often, the problem is not just what you hear in your own head, it's what you hear from others as well. Who gives you most of your advice? Your mother, your older sisters and your friends, right? Are these the same people who are *in* relationships, but complain constantly about one thing or another they wish was different in their own lives?

My dad was a life coach and he was awesome at it, so I grew up knowing how to take charge of my own thoughts and behaviors. He taught me the value of believing in myself and helping others. The problem for my dad was that he was clueless when it came to love. Since he was my dad, though, I trusted him when it came to women. I later learned the error of my ways.

Listening to the advice of others is only beneficial if they truly know what they're talking about. If, however, the only qualification of someone dosing out advice is that they're in a relationship, I'd take it with a grain of salt.

Some people are truly skilled at helping you with your relationship. If you don't choose me, choose another relationship or life coach. Just please choose someone who knows what they're talking about. That's all I ask.

If you were to take golf lessons from me, you'd be making a huge mistake, but if you allow me to help you through this challenging time in your life, you'll be making one of the best moves of your life. Your friends and family genuinely want you to be happy. I don't doubt that, but their advice is skewed. They're giving you advice through their own lenses, not yours.

Listening to my dad when it came to issues of the heart was a huge mistake for me. I learned that lesson the hard way. He meant well but his track record wasn't all that hot. My parents divorced when I was 15. He really didn't have *that* much figured out.

## It's Only Partially About Success

Many women I work with are successful businesswomen, sometimes owners of their own businesses. They want to approach dating with the same vigor they give to their career. They are intense and often have a plan to put their head down and not stop until they find Mr. Right. It can become their sole focus.

While you are reading a book on how to be single and happy, I know that, deep down inside, you don't want to be single. Of course, you do want to be happy, so what I'd like to suggest to you is my theory – you can't be happy as part of a couple until you're happy being just you.

Certainly, if you spend every night hanging out in various venues, you will eventually meet some men – maybe even some great men. The odds are in your favor, but is this how you want to spend every evening of your life?

*You come home from a long day at work, change clothes into something a little more man-hunting appropriate, and go out to a bar, pub, wine tasting, charity event, or who knows what. You bat your eyes at dozens of men, flash them a smile, and hope for the best.*

Does this sound like what you want to experience day after day? Of course not! Most of that won't work anyway!

## Create *Your* Story

Instead of focusing your energy on finding love, focus your energy on building your story. We all have a story, and everyone's story is different. My story includes things like playing hockey as a kid, suffering through my parents' divorce, growing up with three older sisters, learning a trade, and then owning my own construction business. Then, I got fed up with the dating wheel of fortune and learned how to fix relationships. There is much more to my story than that, but nobody else has *my* story.

Your story includes the things you have experienced in your life so far. Young or old, you have a story. Regardless of what your story is today, the last chapter has not yet been written. In fact, never say you've written the last chapter. Just keep piling them on, one after another.

Remember Frodo in *The Lord of the Rings?* At the very end, Frodo hands his diary to his friend Samwise right before he sails off. Frodo told him to write his own ending.

**That's what I would love for you to do!**

Today begins a new chapter of your story. A grand story! The things you include in your next chapter will center around working toward those dreams you've always had. And now, you are armed with the tools to conquer your goals because you are attacking the limiting beliefs that have been stopping you.

Each day, wake up and decide how you can add to your story! It might be something as simple as trying a wild flavor of coffee or getting brave and signing up for a MeetUp that helps you face one of your fears. Yesterday, mine was calling an old high school friend with whom I had a falling out twenty years ago. I was afraid to call him.

Guess what? We are friends again! Come to find out he was too afraid to call me too.

### Screw you limiting beliefs!

When you meet people, whether it's a new female friend, a potential boss or a man, your story will be the thing that piques their interest. If I'm hiring a new employee, I'd much rather hire someone who is adventurous and faces challenges head-on than someone who sits shivering in their living room with a tub of ice cream and a spoon.

I want to date the woman who embraces life, conquers her fears, and lives each day to the fullest. I'm not alone.

Who is the woman you want to be? That is the person to embrace. That's the story you want to build.

## Recognize Where Your Thoughts Originate

As much as we would like to take credit for conjuring up every single thought we have, the truth is that many of the thoughts we have originate outside of our own minds. The easiest example is when you turn on the television while you're getting ready for work, and what does the weatherman say? "It's going to be a dreary day today."

He doesn't mean to set you on a course of having a dreary day, but he just input that into your mind, whether you even realized it or not. Now, someone at work will say something like, "*How's your day going?*" and you'll reply with, "*Oh, it's such a dreary day, I'm just trying to get through it so I can go home and relax.*" You probably think you came up with that all on your own, but in truth, the weatherman unknowingly planted that seed while you were putting on your makeup.

Many of the limiting beliefs you have originated somewhere else. They might have come from how your parents spoke to you, or to one another. They might come from words hissed at you by an insensitive teacher or a coach who was particularly harsh. An ex-beau could have said something that stuck in your mind, or even a friend. If you were bullied in any way by anyone, those beliefs have most likely set in.

## Identify Judgment and Commit to Change

The problem with the beliefs you've identified is that most of them are judgmental. We not only fear the judgment of others, but we inflict judgment on ourselves, often based on what we perceive others are saying. I think women are particularly good at this, although men do it too.

Most of the time, it is true that whatever negatives you see in someone else are the same negatives you see in your own self, and hate the most about yourself. A friend was sharing with me a story about her mother the other day.

*Betty has convinced herself that her sister, Carla, is angry with her. It's something she conjured up in her head, based on the fact that when Betty called Carla on her birthday, Carla didn't answer. Betty concluded Carla is angry with her and even rolled out a conjured-up reason for this anger.*

*Six months later Betty is talking to my friend. She's complaining about how fake her sister is, saying, "I hate how Carla goes into a room, smiling at everyone as if she's their best friend, talking to everyone, being so nice. Then, as soon as she's away from them, all she does is complain about every one of them."*

*All my friend can think is how much this sounds like Betty, not Carla! Betty has taken the things about herself that she likes the least and projected them onto her sister, instead.*

We are all judgmental. It's human nature. The trick is to begin to recognize when you're doing it and stop! This type of behavior causes you to feel anxious, depressed, discouraged, unmotivated and frustrated, to name a few. Do these sound familiar?

Rather than letting those judgmental thoughts ride, put a stop to them and try to unearth the dirt around them. Let curiosity take over. Ask yourself what you're feeling at that moment. What is that feeling trying to tell you? Become an investigator, rather than a judge. Ask yourself how this judgmental thought is helping you. Odds are it's not helping you at all. Look for the root cause of that thought. Who told you this first? Why do you believe it? Is it really true?

If your judgment is falling on someone else, ask yourself what it is about what they're doing that truly bothers you so much. Do you feel threatened? Does it tear at a big fear you have? Do you feel jealous of that person?

Instead of comparing yourself to someone else, consider how you can be a better version of you than you were yesterday. What can you do today to improve?

Think about your own future. You've laid out some great dreams if you've done the *Single Steps* from the free workbook. Envision yourself five years down the line – how many of those dreams are in place? What does that feel like?

# CHAPTER 5 ACTION STEPS

- Write your story, as it is today, regardless of what it says

- Identify the story you want to begin building

- Identify the source of some of your self-limiting beliefs

- Begin to overcome your judgmental thoughts; identify the true source

# Chapter 6: Living in the Past (The One Who Got Away)

Most everyone can tell some version of this story. Let's see if it rings true for you:

*I met this guy in my first week of college. He was great – the quint-essential tall dark and handsome type. We went out a few times, but I found myself turned off by his lack of commitment to his studies. He told me he was in college because his parents forced him to go, not because he wanted to be there. His focus was on his soccer career. He was good and played on the college team, but it turned out to be his whole life. I broke things off because I wanted someone committed to a 'real' career, not a dream.*

*Now, a few years later, he's playing on a professional team in England. He gets to travel all over the world and, as my luck would have it, he's even more handsome than he was in college. I heard his team was coming to play in a nearby town, so I decided to try and connect with him. I found him on social media, only to discover he has a beautiful wife and a small child.*

*What was I thinking when I broke up with him? That could be me! I could be the wife in England with a small child, married to the handsome guy. Instead, I'm stuck in a job I don't even like, living with a roommate who doesn't know what the word clean means, and paying student loans, and, to add insult to injury, I'm SINGLE! I blew it!*

Your story might vary some, but we all have the story of the *one who got away*. The story isn't the problem. What you tell yourself about the story, and how you allow it to impact your life can be the problem.

Life is full of regrets:

- I should have studied business instead of science in college

- I should have passed on the second chocolate donut for breakfast

- I shouldn't have bought those new red shoes

For the most part, we move on. We're just stuck in a crappy moment where everything feels like it's gone to pot. The only time this is problematic is when you fixate on the should'a-could'a-would'a moments instead of what lies before you.

In fact, I will argue that you can't see the future if you're always looking in your past. It's like driving down the road looking in the rearview mirror. Eventually, you're going to crash.

In the story above, the woman telling it is imagining that if she had stayed with that guy, they would have been together throughout college and his early soccer days when things were tough. She imagines that not breaking up with him like she did would have had a happy ending. Not only that, but she imagines that this is *the only* happy ending she could possibly have.

This is your emotional mind hard at work. You're bummed about your life, feeling particularly lonely and maybe even afraid. This is causing you to feel stressed, anxious and miserable. Feeling this way stops you from embracing where you are right now.

My only question is this – where did you develop this insight to know how things would have gone? How can you guarantee that if you had done something differently, the outcome would be what you envision right now?

You can't. Let me hear you say it... come on, you can do it – I'll say it with you, "*I can't.*" I can't either. I have a ton of 'what ifs' in life too. What if I stayed in school? What if I took that job in LA?

The good thing is if you're living with regrets, it means you've been living and not hiding under a rock or playing it safe. When someone tells me they have no regrets in their life, I wonder what on earth they've done. They couldn't have tried anything new, dated anyone or taken any risks.

## Types of Regret

There are several ways in which regret can creep into your life. Let's look at a few.

### You Regret Something You Said or Did to Someone Else

When you are angry, words you wish you could suck right back in come out anyway. Sometimes you realize it immediately, other times, you realize later.

There was a great story floating around social media a while back. While I'm sure it was fabricated, the message is worth repeating.

*A man was frustrated with how often his son said hurtful things to his siblings or friends, so one morning, the dad told his son to go out and pound as many nails as he could find into their old wooden fence. The son went out and pounded in a ton of nails and came back in.*

*The next morning, the father told his son to go out and remove the nails. After 30 minutes and just a few nails removed, the son was frustrated and complaining to his dad, "I can't get them out!"*

*Dad quickly landed his message. Consider each of those nails to be words you've said to someone else. They're easy to pound in but very difficult to take back.*

Whether someone said something to you, or you said something to another person, those words tend to stick. You hear them reverberating over and over in your head. They drag you down like a giant lead weight.

If possible, extend an apology and ask forgiveness. If the words were said to you, extend forgiveness to the person speaking them, even if it's just in your head. Look at it this way, regretting this hurtful exchange means you care. That's a good thing!

### Regret for Something You Did

Perhaps it's that breakup you're regretting, or maybe it's not buying that shiny red car when you saw it. Maybe you regret saying yes to someone when they asked for help.

Regardless of the cause, the result is the same. You have envisioned a brighter outcome than the one you've experienced. You imagine that if you'd made a different choice, everything would be perfect.

You become attached to the vision of perfection you never realized, rather than dealing with the outcome.

To overcome this regret, look at how you want to feel, how you want your world to be, and how you want to express yourself, and move forward with those things. Leave behind the rest. It serves you no purpose. There is no reason you can't carry forward happy feelings, even though the outcome wasn't what you wanted it to be.

### Regret for a Missed Opportunity

Nobody gets to the end of their life and regrets the lessons they've learned through the mistakes they've made. People get to the end of their life and regret missed opportunities. They regret the chances they had to do something unique, risky, kind or even challenging.

Rather than live with regret for things you've allowed to pass by, consider each opportunity carefully. This can be very difficult if something is particularly risky or strikes a lot of fear inside you, but that's all the more reason to consider taking the leap!

Heather wrote to me once, explaining her regret:

*A good friend won two tickets to Hawaii and since neither of us was dating someone, he asked me to go with him. I initially agreed, but by the time the trip came, I was dating someone and thought it would be weird to go on the trip with another man, even though we were just friends, so I passed.*

*Of course, now I'm not seeing that man and I wish I had gone on the trip. I regret so much missing that chance to go somewhere I really wanted to go. Now, I have no guy and no trip.*

Heather will always wonder what would have been different in her life if she had taken that trip. In some way, she may even hold a grudge against the guy she was dating, even though he never even knew about the opportunity.

Consider carefully the opportunities which come your way, now, when you are single and think even more carefully about saying no to them. You may never get another chance to leap at something. Go for it. It could change your life in a way you may never know!

### Regret for Not Being Where You Want to Be

At some point in life, many people wake up and realize they aren't where they thought they would be at that time. As a younger person, they imagined a much different reality than the one they face.

*Why didn't I take that higher paying job? I know now I could have handled it!*

*Why didn't I go out with that guy again? He was awesome, but I was terrified!*

Perhaps you've allowed your values to become less important to you. Someone or something has come into your life, and you've let go of what matters to you. You stopped going to church, or you quit volunteering for Special Olympics.

Facing this type of regret means it's time for recalibration. Sit down and determine what your values are, and what you can do to live true to them. This is a *huge* cause of unhappiness for many people and often, people tend to allow relationships to cloud their values.

After the relationship ends, they have trouble finding their way back to their values. While some of our values do change as our life advances, many do not. It's important for you to determine what your values are today, and how you can live your life true to yourself.

### Sadness and Shame – They're Not Really Regret

When you feel sad, you're mourning a loss of something. When you feel regret, you're mourning a poor behavior choice. Still, many will feel sad and think they should feel regret.

Loss is a part of life. We lose loved ones, we lose jobs, we lose car keys. Each carries a different feeling of sadness, anger or frustration. None of those things should lead you to regret.

Allow yourself to feel the sadness of loss. Let those feelings flow through you and experience them. Don't allow them to consume you or drag you into regretful thinking (wallowing).

Shame is a different creature. When you feel ashamed, you feel small, not good enough, less than adequate. Shame makes you wish something hadn't happened. Perhaps when you regret something, you are ashamed of your own behavior.

It's important to understand that shame can continue to grow and build you into someone who feels less and less confident.

Turn your language around and believe this one truth in life – you *are* worthy of love, you *are* good enough. Boot anyone who tells you something different out of your life!

## What Regret Does to You

Regret can really mess with your life. Your unhappiness may, in some way, be rooted to some regret, perhaps over a man, but maybe over a missed opportunity, words you said that you wish you could take back or any number of other things.

We've been talking about it for a while, but what exactly is regret? Merriam-Webster defines regret this way:

*Sorrow aroused by circumstances beyond one's control or power to repair; an expression of distressing emotion (such as sorrow).*

The important words in that definition might be "beyond one's control to repair." Whether it was once under your control to repair what happened or not, the truth is that now, there is often little that can be done to change what happened.

Generally speaking, regret involves blaming yourself for a negative outcome. You wish you had made a different choice at some point in the past.

As you might guess, this sounds an awful lot like that chapter on rumination, as well it should. Regrets can lead to ruminating. Regret and/or rumination can cause depression and chronic[4] (long-term) stress. Stress in your body, over an extended period of time, can have physiological side effects[5] on your heart and circulatory system in general.

Regret also hinders your ability to move forward. Your mind is swarming with negative thoughts – many of them self-deprecating. You are the cause of all your misery; you alone shoulder the blame for every mistake that has crossed your path for your entire life. You tell yourself you're worthless, dumb, or any host of negative adjectives.

## Turning Regret Around

There is good news! You can change this course. How?

*I'm so happy you asked!*

### What is Your Regret Telling You?

Regret carries an important message, a sort of 'look before you leap' type of message. Often, when we have regret over something, it's because something was done too quickly, without careful consideration of all the ramifications of the final decision.

One way to turn around your parade of regret is to use this realization to think more carefully about decisions in the future. Take an extra day or two to think something through. The bigger the decision, the more thought you should give it.

But, not to an extreme. Find the balance between taking the time to think something through, and its negative companion, overthinking your decision.

### Striking the Balance

*"Okay, Gregg, fine but how do I strike a balance between not thinking enough and thinking too much about something?"*

Don't become one of those people who can't make a decision. That's just a lack of confidence in the opposite direction, not an improvement. Instead, let me give you a few suggestions that might help.

### Pay Attention to When You Might Be Thinking Too Much

If you keep replaying something over and over, you're thinking too much about it. You're either ruminating (fretting over something from the past) or worrying (playing out your own version of what *might* happen in the future).

Most of us are great at anticipating a future negative:

*If I click "Like" on this guy's online profile, he will send me an email, and I'll be stuck emailing with him. He might turn out to be a jerk and then, there I am, emailing back and forth with a jerk. Next thing you know, I'll have to go out with him on a date. Will he even show up? Geeze that will be terrible – sitting there alone, waiting for someone who's never going to show.*

Man, I'm anxious just thinking about it! The truth is you've over-thought the whole thing. Instead, this might work better: *I can click "Like" on this guy's online profile. If he reaches out, I can learn more about him and maybe go out on a date if he seems nice.*

Yes, they're both future projections but one is more realistic than the other. The first one anticipates a doomsday type of ending, while the other just says let's see what happens.

### Challenge What You Think

Instead of conjuring up the worst possible outcome, look for these future falsehoods and challenge them. If you agree to a first date with a new guy, do you know for sure he won't show up? You've read this before. Look for evidence in your own life to refute this lie. If you take that class in statistics, how do you know you'll fail?

Often, what we think can be based more on fear than reality. Just take a moment to challenge the thoughts you're having and make a correction into something that has some truth behind it.

### Instead of Dwelling on the Problem, Focus on Uncovering the Solution

Just ruminating won't solve a thing. It's soooo much easier to sit there and say your life sucks than it is to actually pick yourself up and *do* something about it. Everyone has been there at one time or another. Even I get in a funk every now and then. Nobody is immune.

The difference between those who focus on the solution and those who focus on the problem is how quickly you come out of the funk. If your problem is not enough money, what can you do to change it? If your problem is a crappy car, what can you do to get a new car? If your problem is that you're sick of being alone, what can you do? *Hint: The answer lies in continuing to read and doing the Single Steps!*

### Make Time to Reflect

I am a **huge** proponent of weekly reflection. There is so much to be gained by practicing weekly reflection that it requires its own *Single Step* in the free workbook. When you begin this practice in your life, you start to take control of what's going on. My weekly reflection involves looking over the past week to determine what went well, what didn't, what changes I can make to avoid those same challenges and gratitude. If you do the *Bonus Single Step*, you will get a feel for it yourself!

### Stay in the Moment

This is probably getting old by now, but let's go over it once more. If you find yourself ruminating or anxiety-filled, you're not in this moment right now. You're either in the past or future. It's much more productive to focus on right now. What is going on right this minute? You're reading this book. How is that making you feel? Examine that for a moment. Do you feel hopeful? Are you excited? Do you even remember what you read 30 seconds ago?

### Don't Avoid

Has someone ever told you that you can't have or do something? What happens next? Imagine the toddler who was just told he couldn't have that cookie on the counter. What's he doing? He's finding the first thing he can find that makes him tall enough to reach that cookie, and then he's eating it.

We don't change much as we get older. If we tell ourselves no to something, it rules our thoughts. When you find yourself ruminating, the best thing you can do sometimes is shift gears. I once coached a woman who desperately wanted her married boyfriend to leave his wife. I am not at all a proponent of married people dating others, but she didn't want to hear that, so I had to come at it from a different angle.

I encouraged her to find an activity she could retreat to when her thoughts shifted to her guy, who had broken up with her in lieu of saving his marriage. She decided on those adult coloring books and bought herself one, along with some colored pencils. She also decided to take on some home improvement projects.

Instead of coaching her to stop thinking about her ex, I helped her channel her thoughts in different directions when he did come into her mind. This helped her feel less sadness and anxiety over her ex.

## *Is There Anything You Can Do to Change Things?*

If you have regret over something you said or did to another person, you can always extend an apology and/or ask for forgiveness. It's never too late to say you're sorry.

If there is nothing you can do to change what happened, it's time to let it go. In this instance, you need to ask forgiveness, but ask it from yourself. It's often easier for people to forgive someone else than it is to forgive themselves.

Let me ask you this – if your best friend was responsible for what happened and she came to you, asking for forgiveness, would you forgive her?

**Then why won't you extend the same kindness to yourself?**

## *Is This Really Your Fault?*

Someone with low self-esteem will take the blame for things, regardless of whether the incident was truly their fault.

*"You've always been a bumbling idiot – this is just another classic example!"*

Take a better look at things. What really happened? Perhaps some of the blame does lie on your shoulders, but does *all* the blame belong to you? Could it be that someone else carries some of that blame?

My friend has a sign in her kitchen, *"I didn't say it was your fault. I said I was blaming you."* While it's in jest, the truth is others will blame you for things they did, mostly because they already feel bad about themselves and they want to make others feel just as bad.

Examine the situation with an eye toward the truth and see where you land. If it truly is your fault, it's time to forgive yourself. If not, you need to let it go. It's not your load to carry.

### Change Your Language

I like to look at mistakes as something a little different. I prefer to look at them as learning experiences. Think back to your childhood. When you learned to walk, you made a lot of mistakes. When you learned to ride a two-wheel bike, you fell off a few times. When you started school, you couldn't count to 100 without skipping 59.

*Those* mistakes are okay in everyone's book, but at some point in time, mistakes become taboo. I can't really pinpoint when that is, but I know it happens. Suddenly, if you make a mistake, it's like the whole world is about to come to an end.

Mistakes help you learn and grow. They provide you with useful information. *"If I stick my finger in that socket, it will hurt!"* or, *"If I sleep with this guy too soon, I'll ruin my chances for a great relationship."*

The key is to look at mistakes differently, to use different language. A mistake is really an opportunity to learn something new. You chose a guy who was wrong for you in some way – what can you learn from that?

## You Cannot Change the Past

As much as we would all like to go back and do things differently, the truth is we can't. By getting hung up on regrets, you are staying stuck in the past and wishing for something that cannot happen.

At best, you can issue an apology or ask for forgiveness if you've hurt someone else, but that's all you can do, and even that isn't changing the past, it's helping smooth out the future for you and another individual.

Let go of your regrets. If you need to, write them down on pieces of paper and tear or burn them up. Just please, if you burn them, do it safely in a fireplace or outside away from dry trees and brush!

What you're doing is getting them out of your life and beginning to turn around your self-talk. Listen for those negative statements and either get rid of them or turn them into positives. You've got *Single Step 3* to help you with that!

Whatever you do, start looking to your future, instead of living in your past. The grass is much greener, the skies are sunny, and the future is bright – if you look for it!

---

### CHAPTER 6 ACTION STEPS

- Identify things you regret – we all have regrets – what are yours?
- Learn to forgive yourself for the things you regret

# Chapter 7: Are You a Victim or a Student?

When life seems to be raining down one bad thing after another, it's easy to settle into a victim mentality. The whole world is against you. Nothing you do goes the way it should. Your boyfriend broke up with you, you dropped your phone in the toilet, your car died, and your cat seems to be looking at you while shaking his head as if even *he* can't even imagine how bad it's gotten.

I can see how you might land here, feeling like a victim, but what good is it doing? I would like to propose that, instead of being a victim, you become a student. Let's compare and see how these two are different.

## A Victim Sheds Responsibility But a Student Accepts and Corrects

In the victim mentality, you accept no responsibility for anything that happens in your life. It's not your fault the electricity got shut off. Stupid electric company rips people off. It's not your fault you got a D on the last test; the teacher is a jerk.

With a student mentality, you say, *"Well I forgot to pay the electric bill, but next month, I'll put a reminder on my phone, so I pay it a few days ahead of time!"* You learn from the mistake and you move forward.

The problem is that when you don't accept responsibility for the things in your life, you can't take measures to improve the situation. Since it's not your doing, you can't *undo* it either.

## A Victim Eagerly Tells a Tragic Story While a Student Builds an Interesting One

As a victim, you want everyone to hear how tragic your story is so they can lavish pity on you. *"Oh, you poor thing! Life is just beating you up!"* This attention makes you feel special, important, noticed.

The student, meanwhile, is out bungee jumping, visiting the nursing home with a therapy pet, and not worrying about what others think.

Part of the bonus of the victim mentality is the attention it brings. People feel sorry for you. They want to do things to help you, perhaps even give you money.

Of course, after a few incidents of this, these same people will probably avoid you because you're a Debbie Downer and nobody wants to hang out with her for too long.

## A Victim Thrives on Drama
## While a Student Finds Other Means of Entertainment

Most men hate drama. Let me rephrase – confident, high-quality men hate drama. Why? Because it's usually due to some sort of problem being blown out of proportion or a 100th retelling of a terrible thing that happened to someone.

A student is out trying new things, exploring her world, and looking for new ways to grow and learn. Her forms of entertainment include watching the sunset over the water or sharing an ice cream cone with her dog, Butch.

Boredom can cause you to do things you probably shouldn't do, like dig into someone's drama, or blow up your own situation into a drama. If you're busy facing your fears, taking risks, doing things for others, and exploring all life has to offer, you don't have time for drama.

A man would much rather hear about your white water rafting trip than how your best friend's boyfriend dumped her for the 10th time.

## A Victim Is Pessimistic
## While a Student Is Eager to Learn More

This makes me think of the favorite Winnie the Pooh character, Eeyore. This lovable gray creature slogs through the 100-Acre Woods with his ears down and his spirits even lower. He makes us smile because he's cute in his own way, but in real life, this type of "everything is always wrong" or "everything bad always happens to me" attitude gets old fast.

When you spend all your time in an inquiring mindset, you don't have time for this wallowing. You're out trying a new cooking class, learning a new hobby or engaging someone in a cut-throat tennis match.

Always seeing the down-side of life can put you in a brutal depression. While it feels comforting to have people constantly saying, "*Oh no, everything will turn around soon, don't you worry*" or, "*Don't worry honey, we're all here for you,*" people don't want to spend all of their time propping you up when they can be doing something fun and engaging.

## A Victim Feels Attacked
## While a Student Grows

You just turned a big report in to your boss. You wait and wait, and he comes back and says, "*This is great, but do you think you can add more to this section on…?*"

The victim feels completely defeated and attacked. You busted your butt on that report and all he can do is pick away at *one* little missing piece. What the heck!?! That's the last time you'll pull an all-nighter to get his work done!

The student says, "*Sure! Was there anything else you thought could be changed or added? I'd be happy to get right on this for you!*" The student saw an opportunity to learn, and also looks great in front of her boss because she shows eagerness to improve.

Constructive criticism is a part of life. If delivered properly, it's intended to help you, not attack you or hurt your feelings. In today's society, it seems as if we can't give someone constructive criticism without fearing they'll wind up in a pool of tears.

## The Friends of Victims Are Victims While the Friends of Students Are Adventurers!

Victims draw victims to them. People love to wallow together, while people who aren't carrying around a victim mentality will quickly shy away from the wallowers because it bogs them down. If you notice all your friends are wallowing in self-pity, chances are you are doing the same.

Students hang out with people who see life as an adventure. Students want to always be growing and doing new things. Sure, they'll slip into moments of frustration – nobody is perfect – but they shrug off this type of thing by getting out there and doing something.

I've said it before, but it's worth repeating. Confident, high-quality men do *not* want to hang out with someone who is a downer, wallowing in self-pity, or always seeing the dark side of things. They'll scoot out of your life faster than you can say Ala-kazaam.

## How to End the Victim Mentality

There is good news. If you feel as if one or more of these victim descriptors fits you, there is hope! Here are your steps.

### Change Your Language

Instead of saying, "*You make me so angry*" or, "*They are always picking on me,*" try something like, "*It makes me feel angry when you speak to me that way*" or, "*I don't like it when the whole family picks on my flaws.*"

In this language reset, you are accepting some of the responsibility for what's happening. You are owning your reaction, rather than implying someone else forced you to respond in a specific way. It's a subtle nuance, but it makes a big difference!

### Stop Fighting Life

When you are a victim, you are always fighting the current. Rather than accepting what comes your way, and making an attempt to adapt or repair something, you're always bucking the system. Victims feel helpless to make any changes in their lives.

The truth is you *are* in control and you are *not* helpless. People often don't pull themselves out of misery because they're comfortable there. The emotions are familiar. There is a payoff.

When you take control of your life and roll with what comes, you begin to feel empowered instead of feeling as if you're just trying to survive until the next thing comes along.

### Treat Yourself Like You'd Treat Others

We often treat ourselves way worse than we would ever treat someone else. The things you say to and about yourself in your head or aloud would never cross your lips about another person.

Self-loathing is a result of years and years spent developing a habit of being a victim. Take some time to dig into your old wounds and core beliefs. What is compounding your victim identity? How did you get here to begin with?

Begin to practice positive self-talk. Stop putting yourself down with things like, *"You're worthless" or "Nobody could ever love you."* Take time to see a therapist to work through those old wounds if necessary. It can be difficult to sort through them on your own.

### Dismantle Faulty Beliefs

I touched on this in Chapter 4, but now we're going to dig in! We often think we know what we believe. A great example is this one, *"I want to make a lot of money."* What happens if you dig into your beliefs about money though? Let's try an example:

You believe you want to make a lot of money, but you also believe any or all of these:

- People with a lot of money are jerks – *"Those Lexus drivers will run you down – **jerks!"***
- Money is hard to make and harder yet to keep
- Money can't buy happiness
- Rich people use their money to control the lives of others
- I'd have to win the lottery to get rich

So, while you think you believe that you want to make a lot of money, all these other beliefs will be your roadblocks, because, at your core, you think having a lot of money is bad in some way.

Dismantle some of your beliefs and see what truly lies at the root. Do you have beliefs that are opposite to one another?

## Practice Gratitude

One thing I encourage everyone to do is to practice gratitude. Try to challenge yourself for ten days to find five new things each day to be grateful for. You might find yourself being grateful for toilet paper, but that's okay!

Get yourself a journal and write at least five new things every day. When you begin to see all the good that happens in your life, it becomes more challenging to find the bad. You start to realize that life isn't quite as bad as you thought it was after all, and things become a little brighter.

## Develop Positive Affirmations

In the victim mentality, there is very little positive running through your head. To change this, begin noticing the negative thoughts as they chug by, and start coming up with positive counterparts. This is *Single Step 3*, which you've hopefully already completed.

Those negative thoughts are housed way down in your unconscious and they are difficult to uproot unless you change them into positive thoughts and keep repeating the positives.

Be sure to include thoughts like, "*I am responsible for my own life*" and, "*I can do anything I set my mind to.*"

## Do Something for Someone Else

I can remember watching some show on cable a few years ago on this man whose skin was like tree bark. It is some rare skin disorder, and this man was in tremendous pain. His body was becoming more and more deformed by his condition every day.

After watching how hard he fought and how he endured so much pain every day, just to get through life, I said to myself, *"My life is great!"*

There are people out there who are truly suffering from disease or misfortune. They are victims of fires, floods, or other natural disasters like tornadoes and hurricanes; people with debilitating diseases or those who are enduring cancer; elderly people who sometimes have no family to come and visit with them.

Find a way to help someone else. Shovel an elderly neighbor's driveway. Take a bowl of soup or some packages of herbal tea to a neighbor suffering from cancer. Find a nursing home or rehabilitation center near you and just go visit.

When you're helping someone else, you can forget your own problems. Being the uplifting force in another person's life helps you recognize that you can feel good in a way that doesn't involve making people feel sorry for you.

## Break the Pattern

In order to find a great guy or keep the great guy you've found, you must **become a student of life.** Learn to embrace what life throws at you by tossing your hair back and laughing at it. Learn the lesson and apply it moving forward.

Become an adventurer. Be grateful for what you do have in your life and recognize that you have much to offer someone else.

Finally, turn that negative language you're using on yourself into positive affirmations. You are a great individual, and some guy would be lucky to have you – once you drop the victim stuff!

## CHAPTER 7 ACTION STEPS

- Be a student, not a victim – which one are you now?

- If you feel you are a victim, go through the methods of ending your victim mentality and choose a few to start today!

# Chapter 8:
## Avoid Avoidance

We all do it. We avoid things that cause us to feel pain, anxiety, sadness or stress. Rather than deal with them as they flow into our lives, we stuff them down or put them off, promising ourselves we'll 'deal with it later.' The problem is that later never comes. We don't want to feel those emotions, so we just keep stuffing and avoiding what we need to face.

## What Does Avoidance Look Like?

Avoidance comes in all shapes and sizes. You can avoid just about anything, or everything, in your life with relative ease.

You can avoid breaking up with a guy you know isn't right for you. This one is hard because you must face hurting someone's feelings, but let me ask you this... don't you suppose he knows it's not right as well, and he's trying to avoid hurting *your* feelings? Ultimately, the relationship will end, whether it's in a few minutes when you summon the courage to end it, or a few years when you have two kids, a dog, a house, and two cars to divide.

It's also possible to avoid painful memories. This can lead to devastating, life-changing habits. This is not only a problem because it can negatively impact your health, but it also impacts your ability to have normal, healthy relationships with other people. Aside from that, the memories *are* there. Stuffing doesn't make them go away. At some point, you'll have to deal with them.

Have you ever done this? You've got to give a big presentation to a large group of people in your profession. Your work is outstanding, and your boss has asked you to do this. You're honored and excited at the opportunity but, in your gut, something is stirring. You're scared to death to speak in front of large groups. In school, you avoided it as much as you could, but you can't escape it this time. You know you need to have your presentation ready a day or so ahead of time so you can look it over and have some handouts made, but your anxiety over the speaking part has you frozen. You can't seem to focus on getting your presentation together. The next thing you know, it's the day before and you're cramming it all in.

This is a type of avoidance. You're avoiding doing the task which leads you to the thing causing your anxiety.

Have you ever held off on an important life decision until some other event happens? *"I'm not going to lose weight until spring when I can exercise outside."* While this sounds well and good, the truth is you're avoiding. *"I'm not going to take that confidence course until I finish school – it's just too much all at once."* Okay, but if you have more confidence, you will stand a better chance of getting higher grades and building some great friendships.

Are you currently single because there is no guy who meets your high standards? I realize you may have already seen the error of your ways on this one since we've visited it at least once before. This is also avoidance behavior. You don't want to date for one reason or another. Not wanting to get hurt is a likely candidate.

## Why Do We Avoid?

Avoidance is usually part of some sort of anxiety. Since we're usually avoiding some sort of pain or discomfort, the cause is not having the skillset to process these emotions. Feeling sad is uncomfortable. Knowing you've hurt someone's feelings is not pleasant. Looking in the mirror and honestly seeing the pounds you need to take off is no joy ride. All those things make us feel uncomfortable in one way or another.

Sometimes, avoidance is an indicator that we just don't have good coping skills. When life got tough as a kid, parents comforted us with favorite treats like chocolate chip cookies. The warm gooey cookie made you feel loved and you forget the thing that upset you until it happens again, and mom arrives with yet another cookie. She was well-intentioned, but she did you no favors. You learned to eat when you feel anxious, rather than deal with the thing causing you anxiety.

When you feel anxious about something, it's because you are attempting to live in the future. You are imagining the worst possible outcome of a situation and telling yourself that's what *will* happen. What I ask you now is when did you become a fortune teller? When did you gain a skill nobody else has – the skill to know exactly how something will play out?

You haven't developed that skill, but it has become second nature to you. Why? Because playing out the scene in your head, with the worst possible outcome, allows you to validate your fear and anxiety.

## Ramifications of Avoidance

One side effect of avoiding emotional pain is that you develop an eating disorder. These come in all shapes and sizes – overeating, binge eating and on and on. Your physical health will suffer tremendously with any of these disorders, not to mention your emotional health, which was already a mess.

When you avoid most things, you are engaging in self-sabotage. You stop doing something or you avoid doing something because you just can't face the difficulty of it. This leads to you not meeting a goal of some sort or another – not paying a bill on time, not working out, not saying goodbye to a relationship, and so on.

When you allow avoidance to enter the scene, you are allowing your fear to take control.

*"If I answer the phone, the credit card company is going to want money from me, but I don't have any money, so I don't know what to tell them."*

Of course, they're going to kill the card if you don't pay, and you know this. Not answering the phone is not going to stop this from happening. The fear you're avoiding is really not wanting to feel embarrassed to say, "*I can't pay you today.*" You feel 'less than'.

"*If I break up with Dan, I'll be alone, and I'll never find anyone as sweet as he is. He's my emotional support system, even if the chemistry between us isn't all that great.*"

Yes, breaking up with Dan is going to suck for a while, but you're working with me now and I don't allow dating down-time to go unused. When you're not dating someone, it's a great time to look at yourself and see what got lost in the relationship. Something usually does. Maybe it's your values, perhaps it's your old hobbies and passions, or maybe it's your relationships with your friends. If you dig in and work to get those things back on track, you won't be missing him for long!

## How to End Avoidance and Self-Sabotage

This involves some effort on your part, so pay attention. Your challenge is to learn to catch yourself in the middle of avoiding something. If it's financial, answer your phone, even if it's to say, "*I can't pay you this week, but I can send you something next week.*" If it's exercising, ask yourself how you're going to feel if you let yourself down another day, because that's what you're doing? You're just going to have to tug on those workout clothes and get moving. Don't look at other people, focus on yourself. It's not a beauty contest, it's a workout!

### *Learn to Sit in Uncomfortable Feelings*

It's okay to sit with uncomfortable feelings. This boils down to self-talk. When you start to feel uneasy, instead of allowing the negative self-talk to creep in, recognize the moment and take charge. You **can** control your thoughts, and there's no time like the present to start!

As the uneasy feeling comes, tell yourself you *can* manage it. You've spent a lifetime telling yourself the pain/embarrassment/stress/anxiety is too much to handle but today, you're going to tell yourself you can deal with it.

Sit in the uncomfortable moment and breathe in and out, deeply. Continue to tell yourself you will be okay. Don't allow the anxiety-speak to creep in and take over! It will get easier each time you do it.

I know it sounds cliché to say gut it out, but that is truly the only way to overcome anxiety and avoidance behaviors. It really boils down to the things you're saying to yourself in your own mind. Listen, take notes, and then turn those thoughts around.

### Pay Attention to Your Own Body Cues

Your body reacts to anxiety every time. You may feel tensed up, nauseated or cranky. You may get a headache and lack the ability to focus or concentrate on a specific task. All these are cues that your anxiety is building.

As soon as you begin to sense these symptoms, stop and take a few deep breaths. Focus only on your breathing. It's a way to dismantle those fight or flight chemicals that launched into action when your anxiety kicked in.

After you've calmed down with some deep breaths, look at where the anxiety is coming from. What was the trigger? Was it a phone call or an email from someone or about a specific task? Did you stir a memory of something from your past? Did someone ask you to lunch, but you know you're broke and can't go? Something caused this anxiety, and it's important for you to uncover the reason.

### Stop the Future from Coming In

Recognize that, when you start playing out a scene in your head, your imagination is in high gear. You're not operating with truth but with fiction. You are allowing a worst-case scenario to play out, and you're treating it as if it **is** the truth.

It is not! Your reality is what you perceive. Changing your perception by playing out a **new and positive** outcome will help you get back to the here and now!

Recognize that you're imagining something about which the outcome is undetermined. You're assuming the thing you need to do or say will end badly. You could even be playing the role of someone else in your head, as well as your own.

You don't truly know how someone else will react. You are assuming they will be angry/upset/disappointed in you for some reason, and you *think* you know how they will react.

Stop and tell yourself you *don't* know what the outcome will be and that *you* cannot control someone else's reaction to what you have to say. All you can control is what comes out of your own mouth. What comes out of theirs is their responsibility.

### Go for Bite-Sized Pieces

Sometimes anxiety comes because something seems insurmountable: a large bill to pay; a big presentation for work; renovating a home. These all can become intimidating if you're looking at the whole project at once.

Break it down into smaller pieces. Break the bill down into something you can afford every month. Break the presentation down into smaller projects. The same with any other type of big-picture thing you've got coming. Look for ways to insert milestones, and then look for small ways in which you can reward yourself for hitting those milestones. Take a hot bath, get a pedicure, or go get your favorite ice cream.

### Examine History

*I can't go out with this guy. What if he comes to the restaurant, sees me and leaves? What if he sits down, but later goes to the bathroom and exits out the back door?*

When has this ever happened to you? Look back in your history and find an example of when someone has come and left without approaching. When was the last time someone sat down to enjoy a meal or coffee with you and then exited out the back door? Has it *ever* happened?

*If I make this speech at the convention next week, everyone will laugh at me. They will think I'm a moron, and I'll be left standing there, a laughing stock.*

Have you ever been to a seminar or meeting where everyone burst out laughing at the speaker? I certainly haven't. Your own history can help you diffuse your anxious moments. Look back and ask yourself when the outcome you're imagining has *ever* truly happened. The answer is most likely **never**. There is no evidence to support your anxious thoughts. Once you recognize this, you can dismiss those thoughts and alleviate your anxiety.

You can also look back into your own history to see if what you're worrying about has ever happened to *you* before. You've no doubt imagined some pretty gruesome outcomes. Did they come to be as you imagined or was there a different, probably better outcome?

---

### CHAPTER 8 ACTION STEP

- Examine what avoidance might look like in your life and take steps to start facing the things or people you're avoiding

# Chapter 9:
# Shatter Your Comfort Zone

I have a proposition for you. No, not marriage. Better!

I would like to propose to you that you don't just crawl out of your comfort zone, but that you **burst** out of it! You probably live your life in a specific way. You buy and wear certain brands of clothing, accessories and shoes. You eat a particular collection of meals and visit the same group of restaurants on an ongoing basis. You grocery shop at the same market, buy the same make of car, and your home is decorated in the same style it's been in for the last 15 years.

It's all comfortable. There is nothing that feels better after a long trip than coming *home*. Home is where all your familiar things are. It's where your *same* life is, the life you left a couple weeks ago when you hopped on the airplane to the Bahamas. It's the collection of your repetitive behaviors, the familiar ones which make you feel sane. This place is low-stress, low-anxiety and happy.

What I'm going to propose to you is this – make a few changes. Stay with me... don't shake your head – I can see you shaking your head. **Stop**!

The best way to grow and build confidence is to do things outside your comfort zone. What that looks like is up to you. It's different for everyone. For you, it might mean getting coffee somewhere different or sleeping on the other side of the bed. It might be redecorating a room of your home or trying new restaurants. If you're truly brave, it might mean trying a new adventure – something that scares you just a little.

Introduce a little healthy anxiety into your life. When you try to live life without any stress or anxiety, it's bland and not very challenging. There is no personal growth in this space. No adventure. Nothing interesting at all.

*Do one thing every day that scares you!*

Healthy anxiety comes into play when you change things up a bit by trying something a little risky by your own standards, or something new and exciting. The trick is not to push yourself too far. If you have a severe fear of heights, for example, don't climb to the top of a 50-floor skyscraper to overcome your fear. Start slowly by doing something a little less dramatic. Climb up a few rows in the bleachers at a football game, or gaze over a balcony in a mall or office building, just a floor or two up. Work up to it.

## Why Step Outside Your Comfort Zone?

When you burst out of your comfort zone, you experience very real benefits. One of the more surprising benefits is that you improve your productivity. Having a routine that is the same, day-in and day-out leads you into a productivity zone where you're all but phoning it in, or maybe you really *are* phoning it in. You're mindlessly going through the motions with no challenge. Everything just runs the same as it did the day before.

When you introduce a little healthy anxiety into the mix, you step up your game. At work, this might come in the form of learning a new skill or taking some classes to earn a promotion. In your relationships, it might mean something like dating a type of guy you haven't dated before or agreeing to go someplace you've never gone, like going to a sushi restaurant when you really prefer spaghetti.

Another benefit of stepping out of your comfort zone is that it prepares you to face the unexpected events that are inevitable in life. When you bust that comfort zone, you're facing an unknown, which is the same thing that happens when the unexpected pops up. Voluntarily facing your fears and taking risks helps you when life throws you a curve ball.

A final benefit of busting out of your comfort zone is that you will become more creative. In life coaching, I often tell people to go hang out with people who are the most unlike them. If you're an accountant, go hang out with artists. If you're an attorney, hang out with engineers, architects or doctors. Anyone who is not like you. Yes, there is a benefit to belonging to groups of people with your same skill sets, but there is even more benefit to being involved with groups that have nothing in common with you.

Why?

Because you see life from another perspective. Engineers do not think like attorneys. Writers and accountants don't think alike, and so on. You see the problems they face and how they solve their challenges. You can take this new information forward into your own life and apply those solutions more creatively to fit your circumstance.

## How to Get out of Your Rut

When you decide it's time, there are a few things you can do to navigate this new territory.

### *Realize You're Not the Focus of Everyone's Attention*

You don't want to leave your comfort zone because you know the people in those zones. They already know your quirks and they won't laugh at you.

I've got bad news for you. You are not the center of everyone else's attention. You probably think that if you decide to dance at the bar tonight, every single eye will be just on you. One false move and you'll be so embarrassed you won't ever be able to return. Not!

Now, what might happen is that, if some guy labeled you as a shy reserved type and you start dancing, he might become very intrigued! Wait... that's a *good* thing!!!

### Recognize That Someone Else Is Already Doing What You Fear – and Doing It Well

There is rarely a time when what you fear doing is completely uncharted territory. Someone else has already taken that same route to the coffee shop. Someone else has already tried to bungee jump over that bridge. Dozens of other people have already ridden that Ferris Wheel.

Did those people die? Did others laugh at them and point fingers? Of course not. Other people have done what you're too afraid to do and they not only survived, they thrived! They grew a little and became more confident human beings as a result.

### Know That a Busted Ego Heals

Unlike a torn ligament, a busted ego heals relatively quickly, if you let it. You're afraid to get out on that dance floor because you don't want to be embarrassed. Okay fine. Let me throw this out there – who will make you feel embarrassed anyway? You! That's who. Someone can laugh at you, yes, but it's up to you to *choose* your reaction.

So, your ego takes a hit. If you look at the experience as just that, an experience, you'll be able to swat off the blow to your ego with no problem.

We are always afraid of bruising our ego. Why? If someone laughs at you, laugh with them, "*Oh boy, I really was just arms and legs flailing all over, wasn't I?*" This can also disarm someone who truly was being mean, and it'll take the wind right out of their sails! Own the goofiness of what you did, laugh about it and move on. Ego intact.

### Wonder What If... (Gasp) You Like It?

Oh, my goodness, what will we do? Suppose you go skydiving to face your fear and you actually like it?? Can you imagine such a thing? It's possible!

What if the new coffee shop actually has better coffee than your old haunt?

Suppose that kickboxing class rocks your world?

Oh. My. Gosh!

You're sitting in a zone where everything is the same, every day. You don't get to find out if you like chocolate triple fudge ice cream because your life is too vanilla. Try the darn chocolate already! What's the worst thing that can happen? You toss $4 of ice cream? Oh well.

### Take Small Steps Which Will Lead to Bigger Steps

With each small change you make, you will gain the courage to make even bigger changes. Each time you face a fear or take a small risk, you gain more confidence and self-esteem. You grow a little. This growth will make you hungry for more.

Over time, taking risks becomes less intimidating and you begin to really see the benefits of getting rid of your comfort zone altogether.

The trick is to go slowly, especially at first. Don't bite off more than you are willing to overcome, or at least not *much* more. Look for smaller challenges to face first, and then go for the biggie.

### *Discover That It Might Not Be as Bad as You Expect*

Have you ever 'what-if'd' yourself right out of something?

*What if I get there and I'm the only woman who showed up? Those men will expect me to be able to do all the stuff they're doing. They'll think I'm weak and an idiot...*

*What if I can't do what they ask me to do? I take this job and they ask me to do things I don't know how to do. I'll get fired, then I'll lose my apartment and my car, probably my parents will launch into another 'I told you so' thing...*

*What if he sees me and leaves without introducing himself? I'll be so embarrassed. The entire restaurant will see me sitting there, by myself, and they'll all think, "What a loser."*

*What if I buy this car, then lose my job and can't make the payments? It'll get repossessed, all my neighbors will see, and I'll be the laughing stock of the whole neighborhood!!*

OR...

What if *none* of that happens. You do the thing you're afraid of and you have a great time, make new friends, and learn something new. You grow as a person, build confidence, and actually enjoy yourself! What if *that* happens???

The *what if* statements are simply your anxiety working its magic on you. Learn to recognize that for what it is and stop the chatter. If you haven't noticed already, this is a theme throughout this book – stop the inner chatter that is holding you back.

### Understand the Value of New Experiences to Your Brain

Your brain loves to be challenged, and it stays young and healthy when you are continuously challenging it. When you stay in the same routine, the same rut, there is no benefit to your brain. It grows by being used, and it gets used when it is required to build new neural pathways.

We all have something called Fluid Intelligence. This is the ability humans have to adapt our thinking to a new cognitive problem or situation[6]. According to the study just cited, fluid intelligence is a very important factor in our professional and educational success.

Fluid Intelligence kicks in when we are doing something new and lowers when we are doing the same thing over and over. In other words, driving the same route to work every day does nothing to challenge your mind, but it will be alert and active if you decide to take a different route. Your brain is busy rewiring itself to accommodate for this new experience.

With regularity, you should be working to break your routine, work on or begin new hobbies or passions. Do something creative, visit museums or other places of historical interest, read a book, set new goals, do random acts of kindness, or a host of other activities that are out of your normal routine. All these are great ways to not only build your confidence but improve your brain function as well.

### Discover How Rare True Failure Really Is

When you begin to look at life as a continuous learning experience, everything changes. You are no longer beating yourself up over mistakes. You are celebrating a new experience – an opportunity to learn something new.

When you focus on the learning experience and what it brought to your life, you stop seeing the failure of what happened. So your new route to work took 15 minutes longer and you were late. What can you learn from that? **Don't** say take the old route. The right answer is leave 15 minutes earlier. Your brain was challenged by this new route. You had to pay attention to road signs and speed limit signs.

Everyone experiences times when the thing they tried to do didn't work. The difference between someone who is successful and someone who isn't, lies in how they view what happened. The successful person looks for the learning experience in the situation. The person who is less successful digs deeper into believing she is a failure. Which one do you want to be?

### *Watch for the Doors that Open*

Have you ever tried going to a meeting of people where you know nobody? There are now groups for anything, some of which can be found on Meetup.com. You can find a group for just about any interest you have, either in your town or close by.

Attending these meetings usually proves beneficial in ways you can't imagine. You'll meet people who share the love of the group's theme, but you'll also meet people who can possibly connect you to other things or people. You begin to find doors opening all over the place. This happens regardless of where you meet people.

Getting out there and trying new things leads you in directions you can't even imagine right now. There is no predicting what might happen when you do something new. All you have to do is face your fear of stepping into the situation and go for it!

## CHAPTER 9 ACTION STEPS

- What's it like in your comfort zone? Think about the many things you do routinely every day; now think about changing some of them.

- Determine what you can do to get out of your rut.

# Chapter 10:
# How Do You Know When You're Ready to Date?

At some point, you may realize you want to date. Then again, you may find a comfortable rhythm in being single and decide to keep going. Either decision is great if it's a decision you make on your own. But, how do you know when you're ready to date?

**You know when you are an independent woman.**

How do you become an independent woman? Keep reading. I'll explain.

I'd like to share this unit from my confidence course, *Build Yourself and He Will Come*. This course takes you from *low confidence* all the way to *ready to go out and slay a dragon*! If you find this unit from the course beneficial, consider purchasing the entire course!

## Dependence vs. Independence vs. Interdependence

Every day, I receive emails from women who share with me their relationship frustrations. Sometimes, it is an instance of a woman being in a relationship with men I like to call wet kittens or men who are not yet mature enough in their mental development to be worthy of a great woman. They are what women might call leaches, losers, players, slackers, worthless bums, and so on. I like the phrase wet kittens.

More often than not, however, the emails I receive go something like this:

*"Joe and I have been dating for a while now and I thought we were really in love. We do everything together. I can't remember a time when I was apart from him. We seem like we were in sync with one another. I give him everything he wants. I take care of him, I do his laundry, clean his apartment, and even walk his dog if he has a long work day.*

*Recently, though, he's been distant. He doesn't call or text every day like he used to. He seems like he is pulling away and I don't understand why. I think he might be seeing someone else! I'm so depressed because I don't know what to do! Everything I try seems to just make things worse. I tried showing up where I know he's hanging out with his friends but, even then he is distant. What can I do? I am afraid he's seeing someone else! Help!!!"*

Or this...

*"Gregg, I don't know what to do. Steve packed up all his things last week and moved out! One day, it seemed like we were clicking and the next, he's gone. I feel so lost without him. I just sit and cry when I'm home now and he's not here. My friends all have their own boy-friends now and they're too busy to come over. I found an old shirt of his and I keep it under my pillow so I can still smell him near me. I thought we were in love. I thought he was **the one**. Gregg, PLEASE help me get him back! I'm desperate!"*

There are a few other varieties, but the underlying problem remains the same, as does my advice. What I find, however, is that some women are reluctant to follow my advice. What's coming next is advice I hope *you* decide to follow.

## Dependence

When we are children, from the time we are born until we reach our teen years, we are mainly dependent on our parents for just about everything. We may earn allowance money which enables us to buy that treasured game or toy we've had our eye on, but overall, we rely on them for everything. As we grow into teens, hopefully, our parents have molded some sense of independence and responsibility into us. We begin to learn the value of hard work, having money and learning new things. Sometimes this happens and sometimes it does not.

Dependence in a relationship means you give up your own needs in lieu of the needs of your partner. This is not a healthy relationship. In order to understand dependence, let's look at a few examples.

### Jennifer

When Jennifer and Mark met, it was pure magic. Within a few weeks, Jennifer stopped going to the Thursday Girl's Night outings with her friends, she stopped going to Yoga class, and she barely ever called her best friend, Emily, just to chat and catch up. She didn't even do her favorite thing anymore – painting. Mark was her whole world. She loved everything about him.

Mark, however, is in a different place. He still wants to hang out with his friends, go jet-skiing on the weekends with his high school buddies, and he spends what seems to Jennifer like hours at the gym working out. If she complains about him spending time away from her, he grows distant and Jennifer becomes depressed. The more distant he becomes, the more depressed and anxious about the relationship she becomes.

Then, he will call or text, wanting to hang out. Jennifer's mood immediately improves and for a couple of weeks, things seem to be back on track. Jennifer is happy again because Mark seems to love her after all. Of course, the very next time he doesn't text when he should or declines to hang out, Jen is right back where she was before, depressed and anxious. She's sure this time, the relationship is over.

### What Happened?

Jennifer gave up everything to be Mark's girlfriend. Her entire sense of whether or not she was happy was wrapped up in the actions of Mark. If he was gone, she was unhappy. If he didn't text or call, she was miserable and sure the relationship was over. When he was around, though, she was happy and thought things were on the right track. Jennifer had become dependent on Mark for her very happiness instead of seeking it in hanging out with friends and doing the things she loved.

### Madeline

Madeline is what many would call a successful woman. She graduated from college, got a job in a hospital as a physical therapist, and had a great group of friends. She wasn't afraid to go see a movie by herself or go out to dinner alone if nobody was available. Then, Maddy met Josh and she fell in love, possibly for the first time ever. She wanted to do everything with Josh. If Josh didn't want to go to a movie, she didn't go, no matter how badly she wanted to go. If he didn't want to have Chinese for dinner, rather than go by herself, she would cave in and do what he wanted to do. Maddy felt miserable but she couldn't really pinpoint why. She was in love. This was supposed to feel great! Why didn't it?

### What Happened?

Madeline was so happy when she was with Josh that she began to believe she couldn't be happy if she was apart from him. She lost her identity as Maddy and became Josh's girlfriend. The once fiercely independent Madeline became dependent on Josh for her happiness.

### Sabrina

Sabrina and Matt met through mutual friends. They hit it off and started dating, but then Matt's true personality began to shine through. Matt loved to go out drinking with his buddies and would often not communicate with Sabrina for days. When he was around, Matt was often putting Sabrina down or comparing her to other women. He told lies about her to his friends and generally treated her like crap. After a few months, Sabrina broke it off. How could she have even liked such a jerk?

A week into the breakup, Sabrina was miserable. She felt so lonely and lost without Matt. Even though they'd only gone out for a few miserable months, she missed him, so when he came crawling back a month later, she took him back, even though she knew he would only make her miserable. She felt happy again on some level because she had a man in her life – any man. Of course, this relationship met its demise again and Sabrina met another guy who was essentially Matt in a different man's body. The same patterns emerged, and she broke it off, only to take him back as well. A few losers later, Sabrina finally sees a pattern, but she doesn't know what to do.

### What Happened?

Sabrina snagged a wet kitten, but being low on confidence herself, she believed all of Matt's put-downs, rather than seeing them for what they were – his attempt to make her feel as bad about herself as he felt about himself. She felt she would rather be in a relationship, any relationship, than be alone. After all, who knew when another guy would even show interest in her? If she wasn't in a relationship, she would be unhappy. Her happiness was wrapped up in whether or not she was in *any* relationship.

### Trish

Trish feels anxious all the time now. She's in a great relationship with Dan and things seem to be going great, that is, as long as she knows where he is and what he's doing. When Dan is at work or out with his friends, her anxiety builds to almost unbearable. What is he doing? Who is he with? Are other women flirting with him? Is that jerk Jon introducing him to girls? She's a mess. She has begun to sneak around, just to check on Dan, you know – to see if he's where he said he would be. She has even gone as far as spying on him to make sure he isn't hanging out with other women.

When Dan is with Trish, she feels so much relief. She can relax because she knows what he's doing and who he's doing it with.

She can control things much easier when she is there to keep tabs on him. Dan, meanwhile, is growing more and more tired of Trish's antics. He feels smothered and untrusted. Dan is pretty much done with Trish.

### What Happened?

Trish's own low self-esteem made her want to control everything about Dan. She felt that if she wasn't in control of what he was doing, she would lose him. She felt anxious all the time, instead of feeling happy and fulfilled. Yet, she was so dependent on her need to control the situation that she couldn't see how miserable she truly was. Dan, on the other hand, has seen through her control and he's ready to snap like he's been fired out of a sling-shot. Her controlling and needy behavior has driven him away. Her distrust has caused him to want to be away from her more and more – the very thing she is trying to prevent.

### Eve

Eve met Paul at a bookstore. She was perusing cookbooks, looking for one on Mediterranean cooking. She noticed him watching her and eventually, he introduced himself. They hit it off. He started talking about cooking and how his grandmother was such a good cook. Since Eve was totally into cooking, she felt they were totally in sync. They started seeing each other more and more frequently until they seemed inseparable.

The problem was Paul was relying more and more on Eve for... well, for everything. Turns out Paul was "in between jobs" and eventually needed a place to stay "until he got back on his feet again." This turned into Paul laying around all day on Eve's couch while she went to work. She would come home to whatever mess of dishes and dirty clothes he'd left around, and his expectation of a 'home cooked meal'. Eve didn't mind. He needed her to take care of him! Over time, Eve became more like Paul's mother than his girlfriend. Meanwhile, her own needs were going unmet. She was exhausted and he was sucking not only her bank account, but her energy.

### What Happened?

Eve liked the feeling of taking care of someone. She was a nurturer and she desperately wanted children. In lieu of children, she had Paul, who was very accepting of the nurturing – too accepting. He loved having someone to take care of him because it meant he could continue in his wet kitten ways of taking advantage of her. Eve had become Paul's caregiver. She was dependent on him to make her feel needed and he was dependent on her for, well – everything.

### Sarah

Sarah went through school basically hating herself. She didn't like the clothes she wore, she hated her hairstyle, and she sucked at putting on makeup, so she didn't bother. She was raised by her mother who worked two jobs to support Sarah and her brother. When her mother would come home, she would be tired and cranky, often snapping at Sarah for not having done one thing or another right. Her mother had a specific way things needed to be done, and she didn't like it when her standards weren't met. Sarah never showed any interest in boys in school because she assumed none of them would want to date her. She allowed herself to become overweight and she really didn't care. She did have one thing going for her – she loved animals. After all, animals love you back no matter what!

Enter Brian. Brian showed interest in Sarah. He saw through her weight to a sensitive woman. He liked how careful she was and how caring she was toward animals, especially since he loved animals so much, himself. As they began to date, however, their flaws began to shine, and problems developed. Brian, it turns out, is a bit of a control freak and he wanted to control everything Sarah did. Since this was pretty much how she grew up, she didn't think much of it. Sarah conformed to Brian's every whim and as long as Brian is happy, Sarah thinks she's happy. The truth is, she isn't.

### *What Happened?*

Because Sarah didn't hold herself to high standards, neither did Brian. Sarah had no self-respect, no confidence. Life had beaten her up from a young age. She had a mother who was overworked and tired, and never took the time to help Sarah develop independence in the right way. She was critical and made Sarah feel as if she never did anything right. Sarah was, therefore, so grateful when Brian showed interest, that she didn't care how he treated her. No other man had ever shown interest in her and she wasn't about to get rid of him. Besides, the way Brian treated Sarah was comfortable and familiar to her, based on how she grew up.

### *What Do They All Have in Common?*

All these relationships have one thing in common: they were relationships built upon dependence, rather than on mutual love and respect. One or both of the individuals in these relationship examples was dependent on the other for their happiness and sense of fulfillment. A relationship where one or both people are dependent will never work. When happiness relies on another person, whether it's the mood or the presence of the other person, the relationship is doomed to fail.

Dependence on someone else means you have lost, or never gained, your own independence. Often, these situations arise when your self-respect and confidence are so low that you are grateful to be in *any* relationship, whether it's healthy or not. If you're in a relationship with someone who is also low on self-respect and confidence, the result can be one hot mess. Somewhere along the way, I get the email.

## Independence

I don't know how to sugar-coat this, so I'm just going to lay it down, right here.

*You cannot become one-half of a successful relationship until you become an independent, confident woman with high self-esteem and high self-respect.*

No way, no how. To take it further, you cannot easily become an independent woman *while* you are in a relationship – especially an unhealthy relationship. Why?

Because in order to become independent, you must get to know yourself from the inside out, and it's extremely difficult to do this while you are in a relationship. You will always be looking at yourself through the lens of how you want your partner to see you. In order to grow yourself, you need to be single or at least take a significant relationship break.

When women are in difficult relationships, I might coach them to tell their partner that they need a few weeks to work on themselves. A partner who truly loves you will give you this time and respect your wishes. A partner who is a wet kitten and unworthy of you will continue to badger you during this time, afraid he is losing you. Keep that in mind as we proceed.

### How Do You Become Independent?

How do you do this if you're living together? It's tricky, but you must set aside time for yourself each and every day. Take an hour and find a place away from distractions to read through this material, do the *Single Steps,* or meditate and reflect on what it is you really want out of life. Shut out the world for a while and let your brain do the work it needs to do to push you forward. If you can take a long weekend or a vacation by yourself, do it, but if you can't, steal the time in other ways.

### Get to Know Yourself

You probably think you know yourself, but if you're here, I'm guessing you don't know yourself as well as you should. The good news is that getting to know yourself isn't as challenging as you might think. In fact, it can be fun!

A great place to begin is to journal every evening. Write down what happened throughout your day and how you feel about it, not necessarily how it made you feel but how you felt.

For example, your sister called and asked you to babysit at the last minute so she could go shopping for a new dress. You said yes, even though it meant canceling your plans. When you journal, write about how you felt about this decision. Were you okay canceling your plans, or are you mad at yourself for doing so? If you were okay with it, fine, but if you're mad at yourself, you need to make a change.

Next time, be stronger, *"Gee Em, I'd really like to help you out tonight, but I have plans with Jessie and the girls. Can you go tomorrow? I'd be happy to watch the kids for you then."*

When you journal your day, look at whether or not you presented the same you to the world as the you who lives inside. Sometimes we try to portray someone we are not in order to feel accepted. We may want to fit in with a group at work who always go out to lunch at a place around the corner, so you go, even though you're trying to save money and eat healthy. When you journal, look at how those two things conflicted. In order to become more independent, be able to identify what you want and also be able to pursue it. *"Gee guys, I'd love to go to lunch with you today, but I promised myself I'd eat healthier, so I think I'll pass."*

### Challenge What You Think You Believe

It is easier to live with the status quo, whatever it is, than to try and stir things up. We often react to situations and types of people out of habit, rather than considering our own beliefs. This causes us to live a life that is outside of what we truly want or value. This can be especially true if you're in a co-dependent relationship. You may have sacrificed your own beliefs for the beliefs of your significant other, to ensure the relationship wouldn't be in jeopardy.

Take time, now that you are single, to really evaluate what you believe. Do you believe something because it aligns with your own value system, or do you believe in it because your friends, parents, or a former significant other believes in it?

This is the time to uncover what your values are and realign your life to be more in tune with them (hint: this is where happiness gets its roots!). If you're not single, you still need to take time, by yourself, to look at what you believe. Are these your beliefs, or are they the beliefs of your partner?

After you evaluate what you believe, it's time to challenge those beliefs. You do this by really looking at whether what you believe is true or false. Let's look at an example:

*Belief: People in control hurt other people with their control ⇨ People in control don't care about the people they control ⇨ People in control are really out of control.*

*What This means to me: I don't take control of my life because I fear being out of control, but I am already out of control ⇨ I need to take control of my choices. I need to control my actions. I need to let go of misguided beliefs.*

Here is another:

*Powerful people are putting on a show ⇨ Powerful people can't be trusted ⇨ Powerful people hurt other people.*

*I have been hurt many times by people who hold power over me in some way. I don't trust power ⇨ It ruins you ⇨ I am derailing my own life by not being powerful.*

When we dig into the beliefs and get to the root, either *People in control are really out of control* or *Powerful people hurt other people*, we can then look at whether or not this is really true. Often, these beliefs come from how we have been treated or what we have been raised to believe. When we honestly look at these beliefs, we can begin to see that they are not true at all, but we are using them as excuses not to act in our own lives.

### Learn to Speak up for Yourself
Too often, when life beats us down, we become too compliant. We agree to something rather than speak up for ourselves. When we don't put boundaries in place, people are able to use us and make us feel bad. Being assertive is not easy at first, but once you begin to feel the freedom and happiness that comes from setting and maintaining healthy boundaries, from standing up for yourself, you get better at it.

Many women are afraid of putting boundaries in place. They think it makes them seem like they're unavailable or they're a bitch, but in truth, people (men) respect you more when you have boundaries. You become someone who respects yourself and it shows. Others won't respect you until *you* respect you.

### Become a Decision-Maker

Men hate this conversation:

*Man: "Where do you want to go for dinner tonight?"*
*Woman: "Ohhhhhhh, I don't know...."*
*Man: "How about that new fusion place on 5th?"*
*Woman: "Nooooooo..."*
*Man: (sighing under his breath) "Okay then how about that Mexican place in The Square – the one that has the fajitas you like?"*
*Woman: "No, I don't feel like Mexican tonight."*
*Man: (nearly growling) "Well what do you feel like then?"*
*Woman: "It doesn't matter. You decide."*

A smart man knows at this point that no matter what he chooses, he loses. He wants you to tell him what you want to do, even if it's not his favorite, he doesn't care. He asked and you need to be able to make a decision and stand behind it.

Not being able to make a decision is a low-confidence red flag. Learning to express what you really want doesn't make you difficult, it makes you someone who knows what she wants and isn't afraid to say so. If you're not sure, follow your values and your passions. One or the other will be appropriate and will guide you.

### Set Goals – Have a Plan

Independent people have goals and plans to achieve those goals. They know what they want out of life, and they have a road map to get them there. Goals help you begin to look at your future and make the changes you want to make. They help you identify what you want out of life.

When you achieve your goals, your confidence gets a boost. You respect yourself a little more and you walk a little taller. It enables you to set a more difficult goal because you feel this new level of self-esteem. The more difficult your mind perceives the goal to be, the bigger boost your confidence will get when you reach it.

### Develop New Habits

With this new, independent you will come the need for new habits. You're out there now, doing more things, meeting new people, exploring the world through a new set of eyes. You may decide to pursue a healthier lifestyle. This will require a definite change in habits.

Tracking your progress as you develop new habits empowers you to keep going. When I am working on a new habit, I mark the calendar each day I do that new thing. There quickly comes a point when I don't want to miss the chance to put another mark on the calendar! I don't want to start over. It is motivational!

### Learn to Take Care of You

Mothers are particularly bad at this. You become a mom and the needs of your children supersede your own. You become so busy taking care of the people in your life that you put taking care of yourself on the back burner. The problem is that if you're not taking care of yourself, you're not as good as you could be for someone else.

Learn to put more of a priority on taking care of yourself. You *do* deserve it, regardless of what your low self-esteem may be telling you. You are important and you need to take time out to be good to yourself. Dress in clothing that fits, clothing you like. Get a haircut in a style you like. Buy some makeup and let the lady at the counter teach you how to apply it. Get a personal trainer. Do whatever it takes to take care of you and show others that you care about the image you present.

### Soothe Yourself

We often stuff our emotions or ignore them. We don't allow ourselves to feel anything because it's uncomfortable. Feeling anxious brings on physical symptoms we don't like. Feeling sad can make us want to soothe ourselves with food, drugs or alcohol. We don't know how to accept and allow our feelings to happen.

The best way to begin to do this is just to label your emotions. When you find yourself wrapped up in an emotional state, label it. Sometimes we just don't know what emotion we're even feeling. It's difficult to deal with emotion if you don't know what you're experiencing. Once you've identified the emotion, allow yourself to truly feel it. If you're sad, feel sad, but don't overdo it. You can go too far the other way. Set a time limit, "*I will feel sad over Brad moving out today, but tomorrow I'm going to the gym!*"

### Take Some Risks

If you've read any of my books, you know I'm a big fan of risk-taking. I don't mean I want you to go jump off a cliff tomorrow, but I do want you to learn that risk-taking helps you grow and become more confident. With confidence comes independence.
What makes something risky is individual to you. Usually the things you find risky are things you fear, so you can start by identifying fears. Facing them is taking a risk. Each time you do it, though, the benefits are huge!

### Don't Always Seek Agreement

There are two sides to this one. If you're always agreeing with someone, you don't really have your own opinions and you're being agreeable, not independent. You're not doing any of the things we have talked about so far.

Equally important is when everyone agrees with you – all the time. Then, you're not really being independent. You're saying what you think others want to hear. Being independent means you speak your mind, kindly, and you have opinions. Men LOVE this!

## Socially Retraining Yourself

What are the advantages of talking to strangers? How do you return to being an adult version of the confident kid you once were? Right now, walking up to a stranger and saying something feels scary and wrong. Or so we're taught.

The advantage to approaching and talking to people you've never met is huge. I bet you meet zero new people, on average, throughout your week. If you come across a stranger you could talk to, you look down at your feet as you pass. The upside of socially retraining yourself is incredible.

Retraining yourself might feel scary at first, but once you try it a few times, you become desensitized to it and it's no longer scary. It doesn't feel wrong any more. What I realized as I started talking to strangers is that most of them like it.

*People want to talk to other people. They want to talk to you!!* The ones who don't respond are either too afraid, or they're miserable people you wouldn't enjoy talking with anyway. They don't say buzz off when I ask them something or point out an interesting fact. They laugh and join in and then, we go our separate ways.

I am in no way asking you to start speaking to every man who walks past you in the grocery store! That isn't what this about. Doing that would be too much and it would never work. Your goal is to lose your fear of people and recognize that they want to socialize too. Look them in the eye and say something you can both relate to.

Do this occasionally at first. Then, try it once a day, or every time you go out at least. Soon, you'll be doing it all the time without even thinking about it. How does this help you embrace being single and prepare for Mr. Right?

Ahh, Grasshopper, this is the key to talking to a new man when the opportunity *does* come up! You are ready, you are desensitized, you have the skills in place for action. You've talked on the elevator when everyone else was quiet. You made a comment at the ice cream shop to the person in front of you about why there aren't more pecans in your butter pecan ice cream and they agreed and laughed.

You have tested what people respond to and don't. You've tried texts to see which work and which get radio silence. You are socially retraining yourself and its working!

As you master these basic communication skills, they quickly mushroom into effective flirting skills you can use with men. Now, you want to go out more and get more exposure. You aren't fighting being single like most women do. You're embracing it!

### Why Independence is SO Important

The only way to interdependence, i.e. a healthy relationship, is through independence. You cannot go from being a dependent woman to being in an interdependent relationship. When you begin with dependence, the only relationship option is co-dependence, which is an unhealthy relationship. In our last section of this chapter, we are going to talk about interdependence. That's what we're shooting for.

I hope you can now see why it is easiest to find independence when you are single and why it is so important. Men like women who:

- Can make decisions
- Have opinions
- Have interests outside of them (the man)
- Set clear boundaries and don't break them – for anyone
- Are challenging because they are busy and always learning new things
- Have high confidence and self-esteem
- Are mysterious because they're always doing something new and interesting
- Have goals and enjoy rising to meet challenges
- Are willing to take risks

## Interdependence

This is a term we don't often hear, and that's sad because it is the equivalent to a healthy relationship. The difference between interdependence and co-dependence might seem like a big fuzzy line, but hopefully I can sharpen that line for you in the next few minutes. We aren't going to spend a lot of time on interdependence in this course because our focus is on helping you to become independent, but I feel it is crucial that you understand the difference and the importance of your journey, so let's get an overview now.

### Co-Dependence vs. Interdependence

I like examples, so I'm going to give you an example of an inter-dependent relationship. In the dependence section, you got a few examples of that type of unhealthy relationship. It might be helpful to go back and reread them to see the contrast.

*Dana and James have been together since college. They met at an on-campus charity event for cancer. They immediately hit it off. James graduated a couple of quarters before Dana and found a job soon after. He began saving and soon was in a nice apartment. He maintained a couple of friendships from college, and had some good friends from his high school days. He loved hanging out with his friends, but he also loved hanging out with Dana.*

*Dana graduated and got a job as well. It took her a little longer because she wanted to stay in the same area as James, but she got a job and her own apartment nearby. She had fallen in love with horseback riding as a young girl and now that she didn't need to study all the time, she got back into riding. She had also taken a few art classes in college and began to pursue that as a hobby. She did a girls' night every couple of weeks with some of her friends from college and had a great life on her own. When she and James were together, though, both felt even happier and more fulfilled.*

*As time passed, James and Dana began talking about their future. James figured out that, while he enjoyed hanging out with his friends, he really loved being with Dana. She didn't complain about his guy time when he did want it and she was still, after several years, surprising him in little ways, like the day she announced that they were going hiking for the day or the time she brought him a big bowl of his favorite soup, the kind his mom always made him, when he wasn't feeling well. Dana is always up to something and he loves finding out what her latest 'thing' is. She's mysterious and challenging to him.*

James and Dana have an interdependent relationship. Neither of them sacrifices themselves for the sake of the relationship. They work together on the big stuff like where to go on their honeymoon, or which neighborhood they'll move into when they buy their first house together. They allow one another the space to remain independent but understand the value of building their own foundation as a couple. Their relationship is balanced and healthy.

## From Independent to Interdependent

Once you become an independent, confident woman, you will be choosing men, not grateful to be chosen. You will be sending men packing left and right! Men are naturally drawn to confident women. The mannerisms of confident women are different and men are tuned in to those things. Obviously, you'll need a man to become interdependent. Let's examine characteristics of interdependent relationships next.

### Both Individuals Have Boundaries

We already discussed boundaries and how they are part of being independent. It is important to maintain these boundaries when you become one half of an interdependent couple. What does this look like?

*Mike and Sami recently started dating. Mike has two children from a previous marriage, and he is deeply committed to maintaining a strong relationship with his kids. He has them 50% of the time as part of the custody arrangement. Mike has boundaries where his kids are concerned. During the 50% of the time his kids are in his care, he doesn't go out on the town or spend a lot of time away from home, other than work, of course. He feels it is important for him to be there when his kids are. He has the other time, when they're with their mom, to do his own thing. He has also decided not to introduce his kids to a woman he's in a relationship with until he is sure he wants to be with her. This is a boundary for Mike and Sami is fine with it. She loves kids and can't wait to meet his, but she is willing to do so on his time frame.*

### Maintain Your Uniqueness

One of the things that attracted your guy to you was your uniqueness. There was something about you that made you shine brighter than the other women he came across. It is important that both of you are able to maintain your uniqueness. Yes, you will have similarities and as your relationship grows, you will become more alike in some ways, but if you like wearing boho style outfits now, keep on wearing them. If he really didn't like your style, he wouldn't be interested in the first place.

By the same token, you have to let go of the desire to ditch his favorite Hawaiian shirt. This is part of his uniqueness and you just need to let it be. If it's bad enough, you can jokingly say something like, "Josh, really with the Hawaiian shirt? Let's look into getting you a new one soon, okay?" Do this with a wink and a smile so he doesn't think you're just being mean.

### Find and Foster Common Ground

In our example of interdependence above, I mentioned how they met at a cancer charity event. This is common ground. In my book, *Pennies in the Jar: How to Keep a Man For Life*, I give many examples of how to find common ground. You can do it through shared hobbies, or things you're both passionate about such as charitable causes, animals, and so on. When you have this common ground, it helps build strength into the relationship. You have shared experiences and memories which builds a stronger foundation.

### Keep the Lines of Communication Open

Communication is key to the success of any relationship. This doesn't mean having a shouting match every time one of you disagrees with the other. It means being able to know when to walk away from a situation, give it time to settle, and come back later in a calmer state, ready to talk and listen.

In my book, *The Power to Communicate*, I provide numerous communication tools which are designed to help you learn how to communicate effectively with anyone *and* come out of the conversation getting what you wanted out of it. Too many times, we fail to effectively communicate because it involves not only speaking but listening. We spend a lot of time making sure we are heard, but we forget to hear the other person's side or from an empathetic point of view. Let's look at a quick example of what I mean.

*Marie wants Chris to fix the bathroom shower this weekend. Rather than badgering him about it, she takes a different approach. "Chris I was wondering...if I mow the lawn Saturday morning, do you think you could work on our shower? I can go tomorrow to get the parts you need so everything will be ready. I know you've been busy at work, but I really need your expert skills to get the shower fixed right."*

See what she did there? First, she took on one of his usual chores for him so he wouldn't feel like she was piling on. Next, she offered to get what he needs to do the job, and finally, she complimented him on his skills. Now, if he fails to do the shower this weekend, her next move is to say something like this, *"I'm going to call Jodi's friend Bill, the plumber, and have him come over this weekend to fix the shower."* Bang. Done. I just about guarantee you Chris will be fixing the shower this weekend.

### Respond to One Another's Needs

While your relationship is interdependent, that doesn't always mean your needs will be equal. One or the other of you may have an immediate need which supersedes the needs of the other. Things like illnesses or family emergencies come along and they must be dealt with. Rather than stomping around or sulking when your partner has needs greater than your own, step in and be supportive. Find out where you can be of assistance. Do travel arrangements need to be made? Does someone need to be taken to the doctor? How can you step up and help out?

### Recognize and Adapt to Change

The woman you are today, regardless of how old you are, is not the woman you will be in 5 or 10 years. This goes for men as well. We all continue to grow and evolve into different people. You need to be able to allow your partner to grow and evolve. In a positive, interdependent relationship, you consult with one another when big changes come along. If someone is offered a job promotion that would force the family to move to a new city, both parties must discuss and come to some understanding. It is important that both parties remain open to the desires and concerns of the other.

We can be very resistant to change, and we can really dig in our heels if someone else is trying to force change upon us. Recognize that this change will be difficult for everyone, not just you and be supportive of the decision you come to together.

### Become Tolerant

We all fall off life's wagon from time to time. Life hits us with something and we take a nosedive. For men, this can be the loss of a loved one, the loss of a job, not getting a promotion, or a host of other events which challenge his natural need to provide or his emotions. It is during a stressful time for a man that a woman often wants to kick in and begin nurturing. This is the farthest thing from what he wants or needs.

A man in any of these situations needs to be left alone until he is ready to talk. He doesn't want to be followed around or badgered with well-intended nurturing. He wants to retreat to his man cave or to his friends until he can sort it out. Your job, during this time, is to let him be. Recognize that he needs his space and go do your thing. Take a class in something, go shopping, hang out with your friends or whatever, but go do your own thing and leave him alone.

Don't immediately jump into, *"He's seeing someone I just know it,"* and don't let your friends go there either. Remember, we're talking about a healthy, independent man here. When most confident men are emotionally struggling, they need you to be understanding, tolerant, and out of their space until they emerge, ready to talk or ready to move on with life as it was before. If a man wants to talk, he will. If he needs your help, he'll ask.

---

## CHAPTER 10 ACTION STEPS

- Define which type of woman you are today – are you dependent or independent? Do you identify more with the women in the dependent section?

- What are your values? Are they yours or did you come to value those things because someone else in your life valued them?

- Review the actions you can do to become an independent woman; which actions appeal to you the most? Ultimately, you should try them all

- What are your fears? These become the things you can face, the risks in your life, that will help you grow

# Chapter 11:
## How to Date and Be Happy

You did it. You re-discovered yourself, built up some confidence and are now understanding men. You've decided you're ready to date!

When women date, they date as if they're looking for a husband. Men date for fun first, and only later do they consider whether or not they want something permanent.

When you go into each new first date as if you're sizing him up to see whether or not he's husband material, your disappointment is that much greater when things don't work out. You've put so much weight on the relationship from the beginning that the loss is more devastating.

This soul mate search needs to be something you consider later in a relationship. In fact, I want to help you do a complete make-over on how you date. Are you game? Will you at least hear me out?

Yes??

**Great!**

## We're All Just a Bunch of Soybeans

What would you say if I told you that we look at one another as if we're commodities being traded on the open market?

Yes, you and I are soybeans. Allow me to explain.

When people look at a potential suitor, they say, *"What's in it for me?"* We all do it. We might not say it aloud or recognize that's what we're thinking, but most people think in those terms.

Who do celebrities date? Their plumber? The guy who fixes the stage lighting? Chances are they don't date those folks. Not because those people are bad or inferior, but because they aren't in the same stratosphere as the actors and actresses. Their value on the open market isn't the same.

Would the plumber or the stagehand be happy dating a Holly-wood actor or actress? I doubt it. He would probably be happier with someone with whom they have more in common.

Is this fair? Maybe not, but it is reality. We tend to date people who have the same equity as the equity we perceive we possess. We aren't looking for an exact match, but we naturally tend to come pretty close.

If you rank in appearance around a "five", and you want to date a "ten", good luck. This is one of the ways in which we make wrong selections for potential partners. I can contact every single woman on Rodeo Drive, and I will get shot down. Why? Because I don't bring what they desire to the table. I don't bring the right level of money, looks, or social class they are accustomed to.

It doesn't make them better than me, and I don't take it personally. In fact, I know if Shakira and I dated, it wouldn't last. Neither of us would be happy.

Well, I might be for a few weeks.

Science tells us that people are happiest when both parties get something equal out of the relationship. It's called the equity principle. Each party wants the best deal they can get, so they look at a person's market value. The good news is everybody has a different perceived value. What might be an incredible man, or value to you, won't be to another woman.

The more positive characteristics you bring to the table, the better success you will have finding love. Combine this with your mate having equal assets and your odds of finding your lifetime love partner explode!

This means that you will be close to equal in these six areas:

1. Looks
2. Income
3. Intelligence
4. Status
5. Personality
6. Inner Nature

*But Gregg, I see a beautiful woman dating an average man all the time.*

That's because they balance out in some way. She might be better looking, but he makes more money. They balance when you assess their relationship across all six categories.

Another example might be an attractive man taking care of his wife who has a debilitating disease. Some might think they aren't equal, but in truth, she took care of him when he was sick with cancer ten years ago, so again, things even out.

Why does the equity principle make sense? Because, in a non-equal relationship, the partner bringing more assets to the table begins to feel deprived of something he or she feels they deserve.

They may feel as if they're giving more than they're receiving out of the relationship. The unbalance grows and contempt begins to build.

At the same time, the other partner often feels they are not worthy of someone with so much to offer, making them worry and lose their confidence. A man might feel emasculated. A woman might feel that she has nothing to offer him.

There was a girl in my high school who was gorgeous but not really all that smart. We'll call her Beth. My buddies and I couldn't get near her. She went on to marry a gorgeous rich guy. She got pregnant and never lost the weight. Her husband started treating her like crap and they got divorced. Why? Because what she brought to the table was gone and he felt ripped off.

Fair? No. But it's the cold hard truth.

Your goal is to keep your equity as high as you can so you can date the best guy you can. I often say this jokingly, but it's true: don't call me if you are $30K in debt, thirty pounds overweight, and driving a '98 Honda that's leaking oil. While it's kind of meant as a joke, there is truth in it too. I want someone better, as selfish as that may sound and, I bet you do too.

Shakira is saying the same thing about me, *"Gregg, don't call me at five-foot-nine, with your money and your terrible singing voice!"* If only she knew how good my shower voice was!

Don't fight this principle. Instead, *Build Yourself and He Will Come*!

Making this kind of meaningful change is done when you are single, so be the best you can be in the six categories above **before** you start reining in a man.

## The First Date

Now that you understand a few things about how we choose, it's time to look at the all-important first date. The amount of pressure on a first date is so tremendous that it can cause people to not even show up for fear of not measuring up. You want to look just right: the right hair, nails, makeup, and clothing are so important you've spent days assembling just the right ensemble.

The guy you're about to meet might have found the first thing in his closet that didn't walk to him by itself and looked halfway decent. He is clueless, most of the time, that his belt and shoes should match – by your standards. He glances in the mirror as he flies out the door and doesn't much care if a hair or two is sticking up in the back.

He's going to meet a woman to see how intriguing she is. Is she mysterious? Does she have an interesting story? Is she driving a 25-year-old rust bucket, or is she taking care of her car, even if it is older? Is she dressed like she's going out after to earn money on the street corner, or is she dressed in a way which leaves him wondering what her assets are?

He wants to have fun. He wants to be intrigued by you. He wants to find you mysterious and perhaps a little challenging. He wants to hear a little bit of your story to see if there is potential to have fun with you. Of course, all men will look at you with an eye toward how visually attractive you are, but to a confident, quality man, this isn't as important as whether or not he finds you mysterious and interesting.

And one more thing, while we're talking about what he's thinking. If you show up in your most expensive clothing, designer shoes and purse with high-end jewelry, he will be thinking one of two things – either you want all of his money or you're so high maintenance that he can't afford to date you. Guys aren't impressed by these things and too much of it will cause them to run.

What happens if we reframe the first date? Let's call it a meeting. Even if you've met him before or know him, don't call it a date, at least in your head. Call it a meeting. You're *meeting* this guy to see if he intrigues you. You're not evaluating him to see if he's husband material. Can you have fun with him? Could you enjoy meeting up with him a few more times for pizza or to go on a hike or bike ride?

Go into it looking to have fun. Enjoy the process of asking him questions and answering his. Laugh. Smile. Enjoy just making a new friend. Don't let the words boyfriend, relationship, or husband even enter your mind. Is this someone you can have fun with?

## Date More Than One Man at a Time

I can almost guarantee you that the guy you're dating, early on, is seeing more women than just you. You do the same. There is no reason or expectation on his part that you're exclusive after a first date. There is nothing wrong with this, I promise.

The point of doing this is to give yourself options. I'm not saying you need to be dating six guys at once, but there isn't a thing wrong with having two or three men in your koi pond at a time.

Try to date different types of men. If you've always dated the executive type, go for a biker type or someone who works with their hands. If you've always dated the tall dark and handsome type, try dating a guy who doesn't fit that mold.

The point is to be open-minded and to try out different types of men to see what type of guy you really enjoy. It could be that you're dating a type of guy because he's almost like your dad or he's the polar opposite of a man from a past long-term relationship. You're probably sticking to one type of guy. Expand your horizons!

## There Isn't One Perfect Guy

If you go into dating expecting to find *the* perfect man, you might overlook men who have the potential to be that perfect guy, given time to get to know them.

When you enter the dating scene wanting a man with dark hair, brown eyes, high cheekbones, and a dimple in his chin who is at least six-foot-two tall, earns $150K per year, and drives a Mercedes, you will not accept any guy who isn't *this* guy.

Sure, that guy would be great if that's what you think you want, but how do you really know? Be flexible when you start dating again. Don't pigeon-hole yourself into a specific type. Don't look for *the perfect* guy. Look for the guy who is *perfect for you*.

Let's imagine your friend sets you up on a blind date. You meet the guy and instead of the description above, he's five-foot-nine tall with reddish-brown hair, he drives a really nice (but not Mercedes) car, owns his own condo, and makes about $60K a year.

If you've already decided that, by looks alone, he can't fit, you won't even truly listen to him. You won't really try to get to know him. He could be funny as all heck, but you're sitting there thinking only about how he doesn't make enough money, and that super-nice Honda SUV he's driving just won't cut it in your mind.

This is unfortunate. This guy is potentially a great guy – someone you might have a ton of fun with if you would simply take the time to get to know him, but you've closed off your mind to him because he doesn't 'fit'.

## Give It A Few Tries

Yes, sometimes you date someone and you *can* tell right away that it's not a good fit. Not because you have a vision of someone else in your mind but because things felt stagnant. You couldn't find common ground conversationally and the whole date was unengaging.

Even this guy is worth a second date because the problem could have been straight-up nerves. Some guys are very shy, and the idea of a first date petrifies them as much as it does you. A second date (or meeting let's call it) has less pressure and you can both feel more relaxed.

With any guy you date, it's important to allow a few dates to go by before you give it the ax. Don't make your dates all about meeting somewhere to eat. Go for a hike. Go bowling. Visit a museum or arboretum. *Do* something fun! Dinner dates are, as dates go, boring. You're constrained to your table and if there is music or poor acoustics, you'll struggle to hear one another.

By making your time together about doing fun things together, you really get to know one another. You learn more about how willing he is to let his hair down and vice versa. You begin to build shared memories so that if you do end up going the distance, you've got some great experiences that start to bond the two of you.

The point is this – unless it seems like an outright failure on the first date, give a guy a few dates before you completely reject him. If he calls for another date, go for it. He's still interested, so why not?

## Share One Another's Interests

A great way to get a guy to fall for you, if you determine he might be a keeper, is to get interested in something he's passionate about. If he's into classic cars, spend some of your time away from him learning something, and then share it with him the next time you're together.

If he's a quality guy, he will get interested in something of yours. Probably not quilt making or knitting, but if you love animals, he'd go to the zoo or someplace similar. If you're into the outdoors, he'll trudge along on a hike or canoe trip.

When you start to learn more about one another's interests, you're telling that person you're willing to invest a little more in the relationship and they will likely reciprocate. You're trying new things, exploring new aspects of the world, and growing as an individual.

Meanwhile, you're putting what I like to call *pennies in the jar* of your relationship. This helps you build a bond with him. Over time, if you stay together, it's these shared memories of experiences together that will help affair-proof your relationship. A guy will treasure those memories as much as you do, especially if they center on something he's passionate about.

## Sex and Dating

Yes, almost every guy you date wants to have sex with you. Billy Crystal cleared this up for us years ago in *When Harry Met Sally*. But a quality man will discard you like yesterday's newspaper if you have sex with him too soon.

So, what's too soon?

Too soon is before he has proved his worth! That, most likely, means the first ten dates is too soon. For the first three to four dates, you're still trying one another on to see how you fit together, *if* you fit together at all. Having sex during this time is a relationship killer. You might say, "*No Gregg, I've had sex after the first or second date before and things went great after!*"

Terrific, where is this guy now?

Right.

A guy needs to earn his way into your bedroom by being a stand-up guy. He needs to pass a few tests and you need to feel as if he has potential in your life. First, let's talk about the tests.

### Meet His Mother or His Friends

You're more likely to meet his friends this early in a relationship than you are to meet his mother. Still by date ten or so, you might have the opportunity to meet Mom. Either way, you want to look for certain things.

When it comes to Mom, how she feels about you will go a long way toward how he ultimately views you. You get Mom on your side, and you're halfway home. Compliment her on the fine son she's raised and then listen to her tell you every single embarrassing thing he did in his childhood!

That's what my Mom does!

He'll blush and say stuff like, *"Mom stop,"* but the truth is that he knew she would do this and he's watching to see how you respond.

Also watch how he treats his mother. Is he respectful to her? Does he seem to take care of her if she needs it? How he is with Mom and how she is in return can tell you a lot about how your own relationship will go.

If this guy is a dud but the family likes you, they may even seriously try to warn you. Take heed. They're probably right and trying to save you misery. If, on the other hand, they all joke around and treat you both well, he's probably a great guy.

If you get to meet his friends, watch how he behaves around them. Is he the same or does he turn into a big player? Does he ignore you and leave you to figure out who's who, or does he stick close until he feels you're comfortable with the group?

How do they treat him? Pay close attention. You can learn a lot about how well respected he is among his friends and how well they really like him. For example, do his friends support what he says? Do they make fun of his every suggestion? Do they follow him, or does he follow his friends?

Being a fly on the wall during these interactions can help you understand what type of guy you are dating, and whether or not he fits your mold.

### Suggest a Day Date

This is one of my favorites and you've probably read this before but it's worth mentioning here. A true test of whether a guy only wants to have sex with you is to ask him on a day date. Morning coffee, brunch, or lunch are great suggestions.

The reason this works is because any guy knows his chances of getting sex after this date are much lower. A good guy won't care. A player will try to change it to a nighttime date, or he'll refuse all together.

The beauty of a day date is that you can have an easy exit if you're early in the relationship. Lunch usually means you have a limited time together before you go back to work. Further evidence that no sex will happen.

### Meet Your Friends

Take your new guy to meet your friends. They are your best defense against a loser. They will tell it like it is and they will see any player for what he truly is. They won't be wearing the rose-colored glasses you're wearing, and if they're true friends, they will be honest with you.

Look for how he treats them. For sure dump him on the spot if he hits on one of them! Otherwise, is he respectful? Prime them with some questions ahead of time or allow them to come up with their own. Is he willing to be put through their tests?

Your friends can seek information you might not be able to. Friends are allowed to ask the more embarrassing questions that just don't seem right coming from you at this point in the relationship. Listen carefully to the answers.

Listen even more carefully to what they say after the date. What do they think about him? They will give you their honest feedback if they're really good friends.

## What's His Potential in Your Life?

If he passes your tests, there are still a few more things to consider. Let's look at a couple.

### *How Do Your Values Align?*

This is a biggie, but very few people take the time to truly examine values. Of course, you first need to determine your values, and there are thousands of resources on the internet to help you do that.

Once you've got your own values taken care of, how well does your guy fit? If you value saving money and he's a spender, it may not work out. If you value family but he'd prefer to spend weekends and holidays with his friends or at home alone, you might have some problems down the line.

### *What Do You Both Want out of Life?*

Now it's time to examine what you both want out of life. Are you looking for the 2.2 kids, dog, white picket fence, and minivan life or do you want to travel and see the world, maybe think about kids later, or adopt after you've gotten travel out of your system?

Is living in a specific area important to you? Do you want to be close to work, parents, schools, or other things?

This isn't a conversation to have in those first few days of a relationship – not serious conversations anyway. Still, you can feel someone out. People drop hints about what they want out of life so you can usually figure this out without actually saying "*We need to talk,*" and sending him into a dread-filled stupor.

### Do You Match up on Living Together Things?

They always say it's not the big stuff that breaks people up, it's the piling up of little things like, "*She never puts the cap on the toothpaste*" or an oldie but goodie, "*He never puts the toilet seat down.*"

This is true to some extent. A neat freak won't last long with a Messy Marvin. A cat person and a dog person need to sort that out ahead of time: one, both or neither?

What about things like the division of chores and expenses? How will you work through that?

Sometimes people just fit together like hands in a glove, but usually, there are a few things to work through. If you hate to cook but you land a guy who loves to cook, offer to do the cleanup after. If he hates gardening but will mow the lawn, then you'll have to volunteer for gardening detail, or plan on having a lot of grass.

These conversations need to happen when the conversation about living together happens. You've got to sort these things out, as well as your expectations before you launch into a big mortgage or lease.

### Take Your Time and Have Fun

The point of this entire chapter is that I want you to change your mindset. I want you to slow down your dating process. Discontinue this whole "*Do I want to marry him?*" on the first date stuff and start looking at dating as an adventure.

Each guy you meet brings something new to the table. At the very least, you will meet some interesting people and perhaps a few losers. You may even make a few friends, even if relationships don't work out.

Men date to have fun. Their expectations at the beginning of a relationship are to find out how exciting it would be to chase you.

Your job is to let him chase you, relax, and have fun!

---

### CHAPTER 11 OVERVIEW

I don't really have any Single Steps for you in this chapter but there are still quite a few important points:

- Look at first dates as if they're meetings, instead of dates; take the anxiety and stigma out of that first time you get together

- Recognize what type of man you can attract, based on your own strengths and weaknesses

- Acknowledge there isn't one perfect guy, but there is one guy who is perfect for you; you may need to compromise on a few things but not big things

- Give yourself every opportunity for success in your next relationship by remembering to date for fun, date more than one man at a time until you're in a committed relationship and begin to build memories together

- Don't let a guy into your bed until he's earned it

- Slow your dating roll; have fun and stop worrying about marriage from day one

# Now is the Time to Grow!

Everyone tells you to enjoy being single – embrace it. Grow. Remember that trip to Greece you wanted to take? How about those violin lessons you never finished? As we speak, people are lying on their death beds wishing they lived their lives differently. They're regretting chances they didn't take.

In order to accomplish these things, you might want to consider suspending the endless pursuit of *just any* man and take a break! Make this the season of **you**. The year of **you**. There are plenty of new opportunities in the future to become one with another person, but that time is not now. You have work to do.

You are capable of more than you realize. You just got side-tracked along the way by life. Maybe it was your lack of financial stability that delayed your dreams, or maybe you didn't want to date when your children were young. It doesn't matter.

For now, you are single, and you have no excuses. Still, your default thought process says you **must** get into a relationship or you're a failure. That thought process isn't getting you anywhere! I know because I was single for most of my life and it was the best thing that happened to me!

For many of those years, I was like you. I felt I was missing out on things! Instead of wallowing, I started thinking differently and embraced being single. When I did this, a funny thing happened. My friends became jealous of my life. Why would they possibly be jealous of my seemingly shallow single life?

Because my shallow singles life wasn't so shallow! I was living life to the fullest. I was doing the very things I wanted to do without anyone impeding my progress. I could experiment, live outside my comfort zone, and **thrive!** My friends judged me, but I didn't care.

I failed a lot, but my confidence was growing so fast my failures turned out to be delayed successes because I realized I needed to fail in order to get it right. I was making the rules. I was clearing my own path forward.

Is this selfish? Interestingly enough, it didn't feel that way. I enjoy helping people thrive, so the act of putting myself first ironically changed me into a less selfish person. When I was pushing myself to find a soulmate, I was very selfish and frustrated. I accepted none of the responsibility for this. I blamed others instead.

The problem with seeking someone who will *complete* you without the proper tools in place is that you become bitter and frustrated with the whole process. The world is against you, and nothing you do works out the way you want it to.

Put the tools in place! *Build Yourself and He Will Come.*

That phrase sits at the top of my website for a reason. We live our lives backward in my opinion. We are taught to be one half with another person before we complete the journey to discover ourselves. This is a very dangerous quest. It allows you to be manipulated by others because you have little to no boundaries formed. You compromise to the point that your morals and beliefs are tossed out.

Then the day arrives when you realize you aren't happy and, like a cruel joke, you are single. Again.

That's why we hate being single. But if you build yourself first, you have the option of **easily** finding a guy or staying single. It becomes a choice to be single, not a death sentence.

## The Year of You

I echo this silly phrase in my head all the time. I say, "*This is the year of the Gregg.*" I say it when I am down and out, and it helps a lot! Last year was a tough year. I had some personal losses. I lost a tooth after a challenging dental procedure and dealt with some tenant issues that nearly killed me financially.

In the old days, I would have adopted a victim mentality, blaming God, my orthodontist, and my tenants. Why me? *They* were the problem. My family and friends agreed with me. *I* was a victim.

That was the old me. The new me posts these problems on a vision board and writes below each one how I'll fix them. I create a time table and think through the necessary steps to move forward. I note how I feel now, how I will re-direct my anger and, most importantly, how I will feel when each issue is resolved.

Then comes the fun part! I write down the reward I'll give myself once these issues are resolved. It's the year of the Gregg!

I bet you have similar issues in your life right now. The same process can work for you. Identify the problem, take note of your feelings and initiate a plan to **fix** each one. Finish by rewarding yourself and saying, "*This is the week of the* ***you***" or the day of **you** or, in my case, the year. I like long rewards.

What was the driving force behind taking personal responsibility for my own issues? I had time when I was single to grow my confidence. It would have been challenging for me to develop these skills if I was giving my time to a girlfriend, wife or kids. I needed to be single to discover myself, my strengths and weaknesses, and the skillsets I needed.

Because of this growth, I became a higher commodity on the single's market which gave me better options to find the right woman. I became an eight instead of a six.

More options gave me a better chance of finding a long-term relationship. I wasn't dependent on someone to fix me. How do you become the best version of yourself? How do you find long-term love? You grow when you are single and become the best you that you can be!

Now, it's your turn. You've read the whole book and you've taken the *Single Steps* in the free workbook. You may have even re-entered the dating world already. That's great! I commend you on your hard work and dedication.

It's easy to fall into a *woe is me* pity party. It takes a strong, independent and confident woman to see that changes need to be made. It takes an even stronger woman to initiate and see through those changes. If you're not quite there yet, don't worry. These changes don't happen overnight. You didn't become who you were at the beginning of this book overnight, and you won't do a complete overhaul overnight either.

Be patient. Go through the steps. If you feel yourself slipping back, shoot back to the beginning or re-examine the Single Steps and begin again. Sometimes, it takes more than one tip-toe through your inner game in order to set things straight, but you'll get there! Stay with it and don't give up! I'm not giving up on you and I don't expect you to give up on you either!

## Rescue Yourself

The seconds are counting down on your life. But you still have time. I have time. We both have time. Every morning we get another shot at living life better. You can be a better boss, or a better mom, or a better best friend.

But you must make the effort. Think inchworm. One tiny step in the positive direction is all you need every day of your life. You can't run from you. You must face yourself to find your weaknesses, strengths, values, and beliefs. In order to inch forward, you must face them head-on as you rediscover yourself.

I get email after email from women who are surviving, but they're not living! I want you to live, and that is the plan for you in *Riding Solo.* Anyone can show up to life. I grudgingly got out of bed, went to a job I hated, and dated people who were miserable, like me.

What did I do to overcome my miserable life? I did the steps in this book. I stopped dating women and I started working on myself. I made a new plan with affirmations and goal setting as the centerpiece. I killed off my inner voice and got busy. I stopped watching the endless bad news on television.

## Reaching the Finish Line

If you want to be happy, what you're about to read is nonnegotiable. These last tips are relatively simple.

### *Sleep*

If you are not sleeping properly, you are handicapping your happiness. There are several things you can do to improve your sleep cycle. One of the easiest is to get on a regular schedule of going to bed and waking up. While it seems like a good idea, allowing yourself to 'sleep in' on your days off is actually counterproductive for your sleep cycle.

You can also try melatonin before you go to bed if you're struggling. It's a great way to sleep without using over-the-counter sleep aids which might become addicting.

Probably the most important thing you can do is learn what the right amount of sleep per night is for you. For some, it's eight hours. For others it's ten, and some can get by on six. Try tracking how many hours you sleep and compare that with how productive you were that day. You'll figure it out.

## Take Time to Relax

Meditation is a great tool for relaxation. Other methods of soothing yourself and relaxing are presented throughout the book. Chapter two contains some great self-soothing tips and chapter three on rumination also has some great ideas for relaxing and altering your negative thoughts.

There are videos on YouTube for guided meditation and there are apps you can put on your phone to help you as well.

## Stop Boring Yourself

Instead of living the same life, day after day, challenge yourself. Go back to Chapter 4 and reread how to create your own vision of your life. Get interested in your life and take action!

## Set One Easy Goal First

In Rachel Hollis's best seller, *Wash Your Face,* she made a first goal of cutting Diet Coke out of her diet for 30 days. She held herself accountable for that time and it worked. Achieving an easy goal gets you started on the path to breaking bad habits and achieving your dreams. Try it.

After that, go for something more challenging. The more challenging your mind perceives the goal to be, the bigger the bump in self-esteem and confidence you will realize once it's accomplished.

## Plan for Fun Every Day!

Yes, plan fun. What will you do today that will make you laugh, smile or feel content? Will it be sharing ice cream with your dog? Will you take a walk on the beach? Can you enjoy a cocktail with your best friend?

Whatever your idea of fun is, seek it out. Even if you just take ten or fifteen minutes to do something fun, you will find it to be uplifting and, as a bonus, it will help prevent boredom!

### End Your Judgmental Ways

While it's human nature to judge others, often, if you can dig into the other person's life, you find valid reasons for what they're doing or how they're behaving. A great example is having road-rage toward someone who's driving 20 miles per hour under the speed limit. When you pass, you discover it's an 82-year-old woman just trying to get to bingo! Now how do you feel?

In order to grow as an individual, this has to come to an end. Judging others keeps you from forming new relationships and finding new friends. It's a signal of your own internal unhappiness. It's a way to feel good about yourself by putting someone else down. You're growing into a confident woman. Confident women don't do this!

### Reality is Perception – Make Yours Positive!

We all see things in a different way based on our own life experiences. Some are good, some are bad. If I see a deer in the woods, I am content. I look at it as a beautiful creature and a wonderful part of nature. A hunter might see the deer as dinner. A painter sees the deer as subject matter. PETA sees the deer as something they must protect.

This is how life works. What you perceive is your truth. This can work for or against you. Meeting new friends might scare you based on your past experiences. Instead of avoiding what you fear, try understanding the *why* behind your feelings. It probably relates to an experience from your past. Let those feelings bubble up. If they are severe, seek a therapist – she can help.

The very process of analyzing your own feelings helps you realize that your perception is not true – it is old and might even seem silly. Now, you can **attack** the fear with new vigor!

### Challenge Your Beliefs

Are you really afraid of meeting new people? If you take that new job will you really fail at it and have to live under a bridge eating squirrel? Are you incapable of losing those twelve pounds?

No. You will survive. You are 100 times tougher and more resilient than you think you are. People who take risks are happy because they have positive stories to tell and they followed their dreams!

---

### FINAL ACTION STEPS

- Define what the Year of YOU looks like in your world

- Determine which steps you most need to focus on to reach the finish line

---

# Wrap Up

There is a lot here to digest. I don't expect you to read through and complete the book *and* the *Single Steps* in the free workbook in one sitting. In fact, don't. Some of the *Single Steps* are meant to take you some time. The intention is to help you think deeper about your life and dig deeper into the real changes you want or need to make in order to move forward in life.

The changes you will experience as you take each *Single Step* are not just changes that will impact your dating or single life. They are changes that will impact every aspect of your life. While some women *do* come to me with higher professional confidence than dating confidence, the truth is that we can always improve upon our levels of confidence, self-esteem and self-worth.

Take your time. Read and reread things that seem to have a big impact on you. Dig deeper than you've ever dug before and remember, being *alone* means you're **unequaled**, **unique** and **unexcelled**! The new story of your life is already being written with each word you read.

Enjoy your single journey! It's one of the best things you can do for yourself!

# Get the Word Out to Your Friends

If you believe your friends would draw something valuable from this book, I'd be honored if you'd share your thoughts with them. If you feel particularly strong about the contributions this book made to your success, I'd be eternally grateful if you would post a review. All of my titles are listed on the following pages. My coed motivational books are listed after the women's books.

## Women's Dating Advice Books

Please read the jewel of all my books: *To Date a Man, You Must Understand a Man.* This companion book to all my books will help you understand men! Read the hundreds and hundreds of reviews to learn how well my tactics work! Another #1 best seller.

Next, take understanding men to another level with *10 Secrets You Need to Know About Men.*

If you want to make sure you don't get played, you need to read *Weed Out The Users, The Couch Potatoes and the Losers*

*Pennies in the Jar: How to Keep a Man for Life* is the ultimate women's guide to keeping a relationship strong!

## More Awesome Best Sellers to Solve Your Dating Issues!

If you're single and looking? Read *The Social Tigress* and *Night Moves.*

When you can't stand the thought of picking up one more player, you need to read *Weed Out the Losers, The Couch Potatoes and The Losers.*

Do you want to learn more about men? Read *Manimals: Understanding Different Types of Men and How to Date Them.*

Are you ready for a serious change? Read *Own Your Tomorrow.*

Do you want to text a man into submission? #1 Best Seller: *Power Texting Men.*

Would you like to take yourself on a self-discovery journey? Read *To Date a Man You Must Understand Yourself.*

Need to keep him hooked with your texting? This is my latest texting book for the older crowd *Text Him This Not That.*

Are you suffering from a breakup? Let me help you with my top seller *He's Gone Now What?*

Do you want your ex back? I'll give you your best chance with *How to Get Your Ex Back Fast.*

If you want to regain control of your relationship, try *Who Holds the Cards Now?*

Confidence attracts! Get it here: *Comfortable in Your Own Shoes.*

Would you like to clean up online? Read *Love is in The Mouse* and *Love is in the Mouse 2017.*

Are you over 40 and getting back into the dating scene? Check out *Middle Aged and Kickin' It.*

Are you in need of some introvert dating help? Take a peek at *Be Quiet and Date Me!*

And, last but not least, for the long distance couple: *Committed to Love, Separated by Distance.*

I can be reached at **Gregg@WhoHoldsTheCardsNow.com.**

Please visit my website just for women,
**Who Holds the Cards Now.**

Facebook: **WhoHoldsTheCardsNow**

Twitter: **@YouHoldTheCards**

I'm a Your Tango Expert

## Motivational Books for Men and Women

*Live Like You're Dying*

*The Power to Communicate*

# Endnotes

1 Baumeister, Roy & Twenge, Jean & K Nuss, Christopher. (2002). Effects of social exclusion on cognitive processes: Anticipated aloneness reduces intelligent thought.. Journal of personality and social psychology. 83. 817-27. 10.1037//0022-3514.83.4.817.

2 https://psychcentral.com/encyclopedia/rumination/

3 Stillman, T. F., Baumeister, R. F., Lambert, N. M., Crescioni, A. W., Dewall, C. N., & Fincham, F. D. (2009). Alone and Without Purpose: Life Loses Meaning Following Social Exclusion. Journal Of Experimental Social Psychology, 45(4), 686–694. Retrieved from http://oh0237.oplin.org:2059/login. aspx?direct=true&db=cmedm&AN=20161218&site=ehost-live

4 ROESE, N. J., EPSTUDE, K., FESSEL, F., MORRISON, M., SMALL-MAN, R., SUMMERVILLE, A., ... SEGERSTROM, S. (2009). Repetitive Regret, Depression, and Anxiety: Findings from a Nationally Representative Survey. Journal of Social & Clinical Psychology, 28(6), 671–688. https://oh0237.oplin. org:2363/10.1521/jscp.2009.28.6.671

5 https://www.webmd.com/balance/stress-management/qa/ what-are-the-consequences-of-longterm-stress

6 http://www.pnas.org/content/pnas/ early/2008/04/25/0801268105.full.pdf

Made in the
USA
Monee, IL